CHRIST
and
Violence

CHRIST
and
Violence

Ronald J. Sider

Introduction by
John K. Stoner

A Christian Peace Shelf Selection

HERALD PRESS
Scottdale, Pennsylvania
Kitchener, Ontario

Library of Congress Cataloging in Publication Data

Sider, Ronald J
    Christ and Violence.

    Includes bibliographical references.
    1. Jesus Christ—Teachings. 2. Violence—Moral and
religious aspects. I. Title.
    BS2417.V56S55   261.8   79-9239
    ISBN 0-8361-1895-2

33, 731

CHRIST AND VIOLENCE
Copyright © 1979 by Herald Press, Scottdale, Pa. 15683
    Published simultaneously in Canada by Herald Press,
    Kitchener, Ont. N2G 4M5
Library of Congress Catalog Card Number: 79-9239
International Standard Book Number: 0-8361-1895-2
Printed in the United States of America
Design: Alice B. Shetler

80 81 82 83 84 85 86 87 10 9 8 7 6 5 4 3

To my parents,
James and Ida Sider,
who modeled peacemaking in the home
and to two admired churchmen,
Bishops E. J. Swalm and C. N. Hostetter, Jr.,
who practiced peacemaking in the church
and in the world.

Contents

Introduction

In a nation whose violence fairly threatens to blow the world apart at the seams and where Christians proclaim that "Christ is the answer," it is perhaps a bit surprising that more attention has not been devoted to the question of Christ and violence. What has the One whom Christians claim to follow said about violence?

This book offers a challenge to conservative, liberal and in-between Christians, as well as persons who do not call themselves Christians but have some interest in what the Christian movement is about. To state the extremes, both those persons who think they can have Christ without pacifism and those who think they can have pacifism without Christ will have to think again after reading *Christ and Violence*. They may find that they have tried to put asunder what God has joined together. Or they will at least need to think again about the relevance of Jesus for the issues of public justice and peace in our time.

The book grows out of a movement for Christian pacifism which, in human terms, would have to be considered very modest at best. Yet the observer who is not inclined to despise the day of small things might see in that movement the seed of something larger. New Call to Peacemaking began in 1976 as an effort of the Church of the Brethren, Friends (Quakers), and Mennonites to cooperate in the renewal of the pacifist understanding of the gospel which they have historically held in common. In a series of regional conferences across the United States they explored ways to respond to violence in personal, community, and international relationships. In a national conference at Green Lake, Wisconsin, in October 1978, attended by 300 delegates, Ron Sider delivered the lectures which comprise chapters one, two, and four of this book. The third chapter was originally presented at the Pennsylvania New Call to Peacemaking Conference in Lancaster, Pennsylvania.

New Call to Peacemaking is not so much new as old, really. While the Brethren, Friends, and Mennonite fellowships are inclined to accept the designation "peace church" when it is applied to them, yet they are not altogether satisfied with what often seems to be implied in the term. That is, they do not see their pacifism as a sort of vocational gift or historical accident for which they should be admired, tolerated, reviled, or excused, as the case may be, but rather as a serious and faithful expression of the intention of Jesus. They understand the church of Peter, James, John, and Paul to have been pacifist and find the church for the first several centuries of its life to have been a peace church. Consequently, they are less inclined to look upon themselves as stubborn defenders of a minority position within the Christian family than to look upon mainline churches as uncritical perpetuators of a deviation from the Christian norm, although admittedly a deviation which has a long (if not altogether honored) history.

Ron Sider invites the reader to look again at Jesus and ask again the question of violence. In this he does what might well be expected of Christians but seems so often not to happen. One observes that Jesus is rather routinely bypassed or judged irrelevant to the question of violence by an appeal to the Old Testament or some criterion of "responsible citizenship," which ignores the facts that Jesus had the Old Testament too, and that He also was a citizen with citizenship responsibilities. If we choose to believe that Jesus is not our example in these things, we should at least be honest about what we are doing and open about where we are finding an alternate example.

The time is right for a sweeping reappraisal of the church's teaching on violence. A mountain of nuclear stockpiles on the one hand and an ocean of revolutionary violence on the other converge in our time to make the question of violence the most urgent Christian issue facing this generation. When the books on the human experiment are closed, will the supreme irony of history be that the nation which wrote "In God We Trust" on its coins destroyed the earth with the nuclear weapons it had stockpiled in its frantic quest for security? It is sobering to think that Christians in America, more than any other group of people, are deciding the answer to that question.

Whether they will rise to the challenge remains to be seen. The growing interest in social justice on the part of evangelicals and charismatics is encouraging. But a crucial test of their vision is still to come, namely, concerning what means they are prepared to use to achieve their goals. What about violence? Certain political/economic philosophies, including communism and capitalism, have made clear their answer to that question in the arms race which now engulfs the world. Will Christians have anything different to say or anything better to offer? Ron Sider says they can and they should. What do you say?

In the end, I suppose, it comes down to how we answer the question which Jesus asked of His disciples: "But who do you say that I am?" (Mark 8:29).

March 1979   *John K. Stoner*

1
The Cross and Violence

The Cross and Violence

I begin with a confession. I have never prepared a series of essays with a deeper sense of inadequacy. It was partly because of the fantastic importance and the awesome mystery of the topic. And it was partly because I have not experienced the way of suffering servanthood in my own life. My thirty-nine years on this glorious globe have been years of joy, meaning, and happiness, not pain, agony, and suffering. But as I confronted the impossibility of doing justice to the topic, God reminded me that He was merely asking me to share as faithfully as I can the old, old story of Jesus and His cross. With that understanding of my weakness and inability with the King and also with you, the reader, I dare to continue.

This chapter represents an attempt to state Jesus' message and example of suffering servanthood as clearly and persuasively as possible. Although I do not pretend to understand all the mystery there, I needed to think through again the foundations for my concern for non-violence.

Christians who reject violence follow the way of the cross rather than the way of the sword. But what is the way of the cross and why do we follow it? For Christians, the cross is not some abstract symbol of nonviolence. The cross is the jagged slab of wood to which Roman soldiers spiked Jesus of Nazareth whom we follow and worship.

But why was He crucified? Was it merely because He came to die as a sacrifice for our sin? Or was it merely that He lived such an exemplary loving life of concern for the poor and weak that He died a martyr to peace, justice, and love? Why did Jesus end up on the cross?

To answer that question, we must recall the historical context into which Jesus stepped and then reflect on what His life and message looked like in that historical setting.

For much of the three hundred years preceding Jesus' birth, Greek and then Roman foreigners ruled Palestine, exacting heavy taxation and imposing Hellenistic cultural values.[1] In 167 BC, however, the Hellenistic conquerors went too far in their attempt to transform Jerusalem into a Hellenistic city. When they and apostate Jewish collaborators desecrated the temple, forbade worship there, and prohibited the observance of the Torah, devout Jews rebelled. Drawing on the tradition of the Holy War, the Maccabeans drove the Greek conquerors out of Palestine in a series of bloody battles and secured one hundred years of political freedom. But that was not to last. In 63 BC, Pompey's Roman soldiers conquered Palestine inaugurating many centuries of Roman rule.

Quite apart from the question of political freedom and independence for which the Jews eagerly yearned, Roman rule was hardly benign. Herod the Great, who ruled as a client king of Rome until 4 BC, turned large portions of Palestine into personal estates worked by tenants—an oppressive arrangement depicted in Jesus' parables. After AD 6, when Judea became a directly governed Roman province, governors were often oppressive. Pilate, according to a contemporary, was "of hard disposition, brutal, and pitiless." His administration was full of "corruption, violence, robbery, brutality, extortion, and execution without trial"[2] Hated collaborating tax collectors exacted heavy taxation. Also the violation of Jewish religious life was an ongoing danger—witness, for instance, the Emperor Caligula's attempt to set up his statue in the temple in AD 41.

That apocalyptic, messianic expectation was widespread and intense in the first century AD is hardly surprising. Almost everyone longed for the dawning of the New Age when the Messiah would come to end the rule of the foreign oppressors. Some texts like the similitudes of Ethiopian Enoch expected a heavenly Son of Man who would destroy the Roman rulers and establish the worldwide sovereignty of God through the direct intervention of God with hosts of angels. Other messianic speculations which hoped for a Davidic warrior-king were even more political and militaristic. "According to the unanimous judgment of Josephus, Tacitus, and Suetonius, such martial messianic expectations were one of the major causes of the outbreak of the Jewish War."[3] Given the common assumption of all messianic expectation that the Messiah would end Roman rule, the Romans naturally took a dim view of messianic speculation and viewed the succession of messianic pretenders who appeared in the first century AD as dangerous political enemies guilty of treason against Roman rule.

And they had good reason to be worried. When Herod the Great died, three different messianic pretenders provoked armed rebellion. The Roman governor of Syria came to Jerusalem and crucified two thousand rebels. Judas, who was probably a founder of the Zealots a few years later, attacked an arsenal of Herod three miles from Jesus' hometown of Nazareth.[4]

In AD 6 when Judea became a Roman province, an underground organization of violent revolutionaries emerged. Full of ardent zeal for the law and intense eschatological expectation, the deeply religious Zealots believed that God would intervene to usher in the New Age if they could provoke a popular rebellion against Rome. According to the Zealots, slaying the godless was a religious duty.

To be sure, not all Jews of the time favored armed rebellion. The Sadducees and high priestly aristocracy preferred to collaborate with the foreign oppressors. The clan of Annas which held the office of high priest almost all of the time between AD 6 and 41 used some of the vast sums earned from their monopoly on the sale of animals for temple sacrifices to offer huge bribes to the Roman governors. The moderate Pharisees also opposed rebellion and the Essenes preferred to retreat into the Judean caves to wait quietly for the eschatological day of the Lord.

The German New Testament scholar, Martin Hengel, summarizes this background of imperialist violence and oppression, so full of surprising parallels to the injustice and violence of our own time, and the repeated Jewish attempts at armed rebellion.

For the unsophisticated Jewish population, it was almost

entirely a history of oppressive exploitation, wars of indescribable brutality and disappointed hopes. The rule of Herod and his sons and the corrupt regime of the procurators—Pilate not least among them—had made the situation in Jewish Palestine so intolerable that apparently only three possibilities remained: armed revolutionary resistance, more or less opportunistic accommodation to the establishment—leaving open the possibility of mental reservations—and patient passive endurance.[5]

It was into that maelstrom of oppression, violence, and intense messianic expectation that Jesus of Nazareth stepped to proclaim and incarnate a fourth possibility—the way of suffering servanthood.

Just what was the message of this Man from Nazareth? Luke answered that question with his programmatic account of the dramatic encounter in the synagogue at Nazareth at the beginning of Jesus' public ministry (Luke 4:16-30). In recent years there has been lively debate, sparked to a large degree by John Howard Yoder's *Politics of Jesus,* over whether Jesus' reading from Isaiah 61:1 contained a conscious reference to the year of Jubilee. A very recent dissertation completed by Robert Sloan at Basel, has, I think, some decisive new data. Sloan analyzes an important Qumran text which comes from roughly the same time as Jesus, that links the Jubilee passage of Leviticus 25 and the sabbatical release of debts of Deuteronomy 15 with Isaiah 61:1. Furthermore, it gives the Isaiah passage a specific Jubilee interpretation.

Equally important, all three texts are placed in an eschatological perspective. Thus the Qumran text expects the economic and social reordering described in Leviticus 25, Deuteronomy 15, and Isaiah 61 to occur when the Messiah ushers in the New Age.[6] In fact, Sloan has discovered that in Jewish literature, the Jubilee text is almost always placed in an eschatological context.[7] Thus Luke 4:16 ff. would seem to demand a similar interpretation. This means that at the heart of Jesus' message was the announcement that the messianic age of eschatological expectation was beginning in His life and ministry ("Today this scripture has been fulfilled in your hearing"—v. 21). Not surprisingly, the good citizens of Nazareth took deep offense when Jesus insisted that the blessings of the messianic age would be available to everyone—even hated foreigners and enemies. Furthermore, right at the heart of Jesus' conception of the new messianic age was the special concern for the poor, the release of captives, and liberation of the oppressed called for in the Jubilee. The New Age which he saw himself inaugurating had specific economic and social content.

New Testament scholars have increasingly recognized that Jesus' announcement of the eschatological kingdom had both present and future elements. Scholars such as W. G. Kummel and George Ladd have demonstrated the inadequacy of both consistent eschatology (e.g., Schweitzer) which discarded or distorted the texts which speak of the kingdom being present in Jesus' life and work and realized eschatology (e.g., Dodd) which largely ignored the texts which speak of the kingdom as still future.[8] Jesus taught that the messianic age had already broken into the present in Himself (e.g., Luke 11:20) but He expected its completion to occur in the future.

That the eschatological Jubilee was central to Jesus' thought and work is also clear from other passages. When John the Baptist sent two disciples to ask if Jesus was the expected one, Jesus responded with words that clearly alluded to Isaiah 61:1: "Go and tell John what you have seen and heard: the blind receive their sight, the lame walk, lepers are cleansed, and the deaf hear, the dead are raised up, the poor have good news preached to them" (Luke 7:22). In the sermon in Luke 6:20 ff. Jesus pronounced a blessing on the poor and hungry and promised that in the New Age they would be satisfied. Conversely, the rich and full would experience a woeful reversal (vv. 24, 25). Drawing on Deuteronomy 15, He commanded His followers to live by the standards of the dawning messianic age and make loans, expecting nothing in return (v. 35)—a command echoed in The Lord's Prayer where He taught His disciples to ask God to forgive their sins as they forgive everyone who has debts or loans owing to them (Luke 11:4).

Jesus' cleansing of the temple fits perfectly into this inauguration of the messianic Jubilee. Outraged that the wealthy priestly aristocracy was collecting huge sums from their monopolistic sale of animals for sacrifice, Jesus called their economic practices robbery (" 'My house shall be a house of prayer'; but you have made it a den of robbers," Luke 19:46). And He drove them out. This was not "an armed attack on the Temple" but rather "an exemplary demonstration against the misuse of the sanctuary to enrich the leading priestly families."[9] Hardly surprising, the Sadducees and priestly aristocracy considered a person who announced and acted out such a radical call for socioeconomic change to be highly dangerous. Hence they moved promptly to destroy Him (Luke 19:47). Within a few days, they had Him arrested and turned over to the Roman governor as a dangerous revolutionary. One reason Jesus got crucified then was that He began to live out the kind of radical socioeconomic reordering expected when the Messiah would inaugurate the Jubilee.

But it would be a gross distortion to suggest that Jesus was crucified *merely* because He offended the wealthy establishment with radical socioeconomic proposals. He called people to live out the vision of the Jubilee precisely because the messianic age had begun in His own Person and work. I am aware, of course, that considerable modern scholarship has denied that Jesus made any messianic claims. But I agree with Martin Hengel that the "thesis of a totally unmessianic Jesus has led a major portion of German New Testament studies along a false trail."[10] Certainly His messianic claims were often indirect and concealed. This was necessary in part because an open, sustained messianic claim during His early ministry (as first-century history clearly shows) would have resulted in His prompt, premature arrest. It was also necessary because His understanding of His messianic role differed sharply from popular expectation. But that He claimed to be the long expected Messiah is, I think, beyond serious question. He took the term Son of Man from the eschatological expectation of a heavenly messianic figure and used it as His favorite self-designation. He clearly and explicitly set aside Mosaic teaching and placed Himself above Moses with His bold, "You have heard that it was said. . . . But I say to you" (Matthew 5:21-48). Thus He called into question the Torah that "to the Jew was identical with the law of the world, indeed with the cosmic order of the universe [and] that guaranteed Israel's election and right to dominion."[11]

Indeed, He went even further. He claimed the authority to forgive sins, which as the Jewish bystanders immediately recognized, was a prerogative of God alone

(Mark 2:6, 7). And at His trial, when they asked Him if He was the Messiah, the Son of God, He said, "I am; and you will see the Son of man seated at the right hand of Power, and coming with the clouds of heaven" (Mark 14:62).[12] It is hardly surprising that monotheistic Jews charged Him with blasphemy.

The Roman rulers, however, reserved for themselves the authority to mete out capital punishment. Hence the Jewish authorities could not execute Jesus even though the Torah prescribed death for blasphemy. But since Messianic pretenders were a clear political danger to Roman imperialism, Pilate was willing to crucify Jesus on the *political* charge that He claimed to be the King of the Jews.

Jesus of Nazareth was not the only messianic pretender crucified in the first century. But He differed from the others in at least two decisive ways. In the first place, something very unusual happened on the third day after His crucifixion (and I'll say more about that later). In the second place, His methods contrasted radically with all the others. He chose to implement His messianic kingdom with suffering servanthood rather than a violent sword.

Jesus' decision to use nonviolent means is visible at every crucial point in His career. At His temptation when Satan offered Him all the political and military power of the world (Luke 4:5-8), Jesus faced and decisively rejected the Zealot option of violent means to establish the messianic kingdom. At Caesarea Philippi, when Peter confessed that He was the Messiah, He quickly hastened to explain that as the messianic Son of Man, He would have to suffer and even die. And when Peter rejected that picture of a suffering Messiah, Jesus harshly denounced him as an agent of that satanic one who had already tempted Him with the Zealot option (Mark 8:27-34).

The triumphal entry (Luke 19:28-40) with its veiled messianic claim also pointed to Jesus' nonviolent messianic conception. As C. F. B. Cranfield points out in the *Cambridge Greek Testament Commentary*, Jesus consciously chose to fulfill the eschatological prophecy in Zechariah 9:9 precisely because it depicted a humble peaceful messianic figure riding not on a war horse, but on an ass.[13] The vision (in the text from Zechariah) of a peaceful king who would "command peace to the nations" corresponded to Jesus' transformed picture of the Messiah.

In the final crisis, He persisted in His rejection of the sword. He rebuked Peter for attacking those who came to arrest Him (Luke 22:49, 50). And He informed Pilate that His kingdom was not of this world in *one specific regard*—namely that His followers did not use violence (John 18:36). Obviously He did not mean that the messianic kingdom He had inaugurated had nothing to do with the earth. That would have contradicted His central announcement of the eschatological Jubilee which He expected His followers to begin living. But He did mean that He would not establish His kingdom by the sword.

But Jesus not only *lived* the way of nonviolence. He also taught it. The Sermon on the Mount (Matthew 5:38-48 and parallel) contains the most important text.

To a people so oppressed by foreign conquerors that repeatedly over the previous two centuries they had resorted to violent rebellion, Jesus gave the unprecedented command: "Love your enemies." The New

Testament scholar Martin Hengel believes that Jesus probably formulated His command to love one's enemies in conscious contrast to the teaching and practice of the Zealots.[14] Thus Jesus was pointedly rejecting one currently attractive political method in favor of a radically different approach.

Jesus' command to love one's enemies was in direct contrast to currently widespread views that Jesus summarized in Matthew 5:43: "You have heard that it was said, 'You shall love your neighbor and hate your enemy.' " The first part of this verse is a direct quotation from Leviticus 19:18. As Leviticus 19:17 and the history of subsequent interpretation in the post-exilic period demonstrates[15] the neighbor that one was obligated to love was normally understood to be a fellow Israelite. Thus love for neighbor had clear ethnic, religious limitations. A different attitude was permissible toward Gentiles. The Old Testament, however, did not command or sanction hatred of the enemy. But Jewish contemporaries of Jesus did! The Zealots believed that "slaying of the godless enemy out of zeal for God's cause was a fundamental commandment, true to the Rabbinic maxim: 'Whoever spills the blood of one of the godless is like one who offers a sacrifice.' "[16] And the Qumran community's Manual of Discipline urged people to "love all the sons of light . . . and . . . hate all the sons of darkness."[17]

Jesus' way is entirely different. For the members of Jesus' beginning messianic kingdom, neighbor love must extend beyond the limited circle of the people of Israel, beyond the limited circle of the new people of God! All people everywhere are neighbors to Jesus' followers and therefore are to be actively loved. And that even extends to enemies—even violent oppressive foreign conquerors!

It is exegetically impossible to follow Luther's two-kingdom analysis and restrict the application of these verses on love of enemies to some personal sphere and deny their application to violence in the public sphere. As Eduard Schweitzer says in his commentary on Matthew, "There is not the slightest hint of any realm where the disciple is not bound by the words of Jesus."[18] In the preceding verses, Jesus had discussed issues that clearly pertained to the public sphere of the legal system and the authorized demands of the Roman rulers. Jesus rejected the basic legal principle from the Torah that it was right to demand an eye for an eye and a tooth for a tooth (v. 38), thus placing his own personal authority above that of Moses. Jesus was dealing here with a fundamental principle of Jewish and other near-Eastern legal systems, not with some admonitions on private interpersonal relationships. Instead of retaliation to a corresponding degree against someone who had caused damage, Jesus commanded a loving response that would even submit to further damage and suffering rather than exact equal pain or loss from the unfair, guilty aggressor. Verse 40 ("If any one would sue you and take your coat, let him have your cloak as well") clearly speaks of how one should respond in the public arena of the judicial system. And verse 41 ("If any one forces you to go one mile, go with him two miles") speaks of how to respond to Roman rulers who demand forced labor.

The verb translated as "force" is a technical term used to refer to the requisition of services by civil and military authorities.[19] Josephus used the word to speak of compulsory carrying of military supplies.[20] The Roman rulers could and did demand that civilians in conquered lands perform such services upon demand. Thus they were able to insist that Simon of Cyrene carry Jesus' cross (27:32). The Latin origin of the word mile confirms the fact that Jesus is talking about the requisitioning of forced labor by the Roman rulers. Not surprisingly, the Zealots urged Jews to refuse this kind of forced labor.[21] But Jesus rejects that angry, violent Zealot response to the oppressors' unjust demands.

I am not convinced (and we will look at this in more detail in chapter two) that Jesus was advocating a passive, resigned attitude toward oppressors. Certainly nothing in the text suggests that Jesus approved the unfair, insulting slap on the cheek or the demand for forced labor. But Jesus' response was to call on the oppressed to take command of their situation in a way that transcended the old age's normal categories of friends and enemies. The members of Jesus' new messianic kingdom were to love opponents, even oppressive persecuting enemies, so deeply that they could wholeheartedly pray for their well-being and actively demonstrate in spontaneous actions that exceeded their unjust demands that they truly loved them as persons.

The radical, costly character of Jesus' call for love toward enemies certainly tempts us to decisively weaken Jesus' message by labeling it an impossible ideal, relegating it to the millennium, or limiting its application to personal relationships. But that is to misread both the text and the concrete historical context in which Jesus lived and spoke. In His original setting, Jesus advocated love toward enemies as His specific political response to centuries of violence and to the contemporary Zealots' call for violent revolution. And He spoke as one who claimed to be the Messiah of Israel. His messianic kingdom was already breaking into the present, and therefore His disciples should and could live out the values of the New Age.

To be sure, He did not say that one should practice loving nonviolence because it would always instantly transform enemies into bosom friends. The cross stands as a harsh reminder that love for enemies does not always work—at least in the short run. Jesus grounds His call to love enemies in the very nature of God. "Love your enemies and pray for those who persecute you, so that you may be sons of your Father who is in heaven; for he makes his sun rise on the evil and on the good, and sends rain on the just and on the unjust" (vv. 44, 45, so too 5:10). God loves His enemies. Instead of promptly destroying sinners, He continues lovingly to shower the good gifts of creation upon them. Since that is the way God is, those who want to be His sons and daughters must do likewise. Conversely, as the text implies, those who do not love their enemies are not the children of God. "You, therefore, must be perfect, as your heavenly Father is perfect" (v. 48). One fundamental aspect of the holiness and perfection of God is that He loves His enemies. Those who by His grace seek to reflect His holiness will likewise love their enemies—even when it involves a cross.

We have looked at Jesus' life and teaching in its historical setting. What an utterly astounding person this Nazarene carpenter was! He went about the country tenderly ministering to the poor, sick, and oppressed. He announced that the messianic age had broken into the present. Therefore the people of God should begin living out the eschatological Jubilee and transform the whole economic order. He claimed to be the long-expected

Messiah and said He would usher in His kingdom with love (even for enemies) rather than the sword. Indeed He went even further, setting His own personal authority above that of Moses, claiming divine authority to forgive sins, and acknowledging that He was the Son of God. What an utterly astounding Person. What fantastically exciting good news—if it was really true. What offensive megalomania and breathtaking blasphemy if it was false.

And then He died on a cross. He suffered the most despicable death possible. Paul's quotation from the Torah "Cursed be every one who hangs on a tree" (Deuteronomy 21:23; Galatians 3:13) expressed the Jewish viewpoint. As for the brutally efficient Romans, they knew how to put down political threats. They regularly crucified political criminals, especially the constant stream of rebellious Jewish messianic pretenders. And it worked, too. Crucifixion had a decisive way of squelching messianic megalomaniacs. Jesus was finished. Perhaps the disciples and some of the poor masses may have begun to understand and accept a little of Jesus' fantastic vision and claims. But the Roman and Jewish establishment did not believe such nonsense for a moment. And they killed Him to prove they were right. Jürgen Moltmann is surely correct in insisting that the cross decisively destroyed the credibility of Jesus' message and claims.

He who proclaimed that the kingdom was near died abandoned by God. He who anticipated the future of God in miracles and in casting out demons died helpless on the cross. He who revealed the righteousness of God with an authority greater than Moses died according to the provision of the law as a blasphemer. He who spread the love of God in his fellowship with the poor and the sinners met his end between two criminals on the cross. . . . For the disciples who had followed Jesus to Jerusalem, his shameful death was not the consummation of his obedience to God nor a demonstration of martyrdom for his truth, but the rejection of his claim. It did not confirm their hopes in him, but permanently destroyed them.[22]

And then he rose from the dead!

It was the resurrection which convinced the discouraged disciples that in spite of the cross, Jesus' claims and His announcement of the messianic kingdom were still valid. Jewish eschatological expectation looked for a general resurrection at the beginning of the New Age. As the early Christians reflected on Jesus' resurrection, they realized that one instance of this eschatological resurrection had actually occurred in the Old Age. Thus they referred to Jesus' resurrection as the first fruits (1 Corinthians 15:20-23) of that final general resurrection. Jesus' resurrection then was decisive evidence that the New Age had truly invaded the Old. Jesus of Nazareth was now called Jesus Christ (Jesus the Messiah) because His resurrection was irrefutable evidence that His messianic claims were valid.

Indeed even more lofty titles seemed appropriate after His resurrection. According to the Fourth Gospel, the skeptical Thomas lost all doubt when he saw the risen Jesus and uttered the awesome words: "My Lord and my God!" (John 20:28). Throughout Acts and the epistles, it is clear that the resurrection was the decisive demonstration that convinced the disciples that Jesus was truly the Son of God (Romans 1:4; Acts 2:32-36). The word *Kúrios* (Lord), used in the Septuagint to translate the word

Yahweh, now became one of the most frequently used titles for the man from Nazareth. In Philippians 2, Paul applied to Jesus the words from Isaiah 45:23 which the monotheistic prophet had used for Yahweh. After mocking the idols Yahweh insisted in Isaiah 45:23 that He alone was God: "To me every knee shall bow, every tongue shall swear." Paul took those words from the mouth of Yahweh and applied them to Jesus, declaring that "at the name of Jesus every knee should bow, in heaven and on earth and under the earth, and every tongue confess that Jesus Christ is Lord" (Philippians 2:10, 11).

Not until we understand that *that* is who the Crucified One was do we begin to penetrate to the full meaning of the cross. The crucified criminal hanging limp on the middle cross was the eternal Word who in the beginning was with God and indeed was God, but for our sakes became flesh and dwelt among us. The Crucified One was He "who had always been God by nature [but], did not cling to his prerogatives as God's equal, but stripped himself of all privilege by consenting to be a slave" (Philippians 2:6, 7; Phillips). Only when we grasp that identity of the Crucified One do we begin to fathom the depth of Jesus' teaching that God's way of dealing with enemies is the way of suffering love.

Jürgen Moltmann has said that "everything that can be categorized as 'non-violence' in the sayings and actions of Jesus can ultimately be derived from this 'revolution in the concept of God' which he set forth: namely that God comes not to carry out just revenge upon the evil, but to justify sinners by grace, whether they are Zealots or tax collectors, Pharisees or sinners."[23] Jesus certainly exhibited an acceptance of sinners so unconventional and unusual that it astonished and offended the official defenders of the Torah. He ate with tax collectors and sinners and insisted, when the Pharisees objected, that He had come to call, not the righteous but sinners (Mark 2:15-17). He urged His followers to forgive others without limit—even to "seventy times seven" (Matthew 18:21, 22; Luke 17:3, 4). In numerous parables like that of the prodigal son, He spoke of God's unmerited acceptance of sinners. He forgave the woman taken in adultery (John 8:3-11) and even prayed God to pardon those who spiked Him to the cross (Luke 23:34). By word and deed, Jesus taught that God loved and accepted sinners even though they deserved to be His enemies.

But his submission to the cross takes us still further in our understanding of God's way of dealing with enemies. Jesus clearly understood that a vicarious death for others was central to His mission. Oscar Cullmann has argued convincingly that Jesus consciously saw Himself as the servant of Yahweh of Isaiah 53 who suffered vicariously for the sins of His people.[24] However that may be, it is beyond question that Jesus looked ahead to His death as a very central event in His total mission. As soon as Peter acknowledged Him as the Messiah at Caesarea Philippi, He began to explain that He must die (Mark 8:27-33). Repeatedly He returned to the same theme (Mark 9:30-32; 10:32-34). And when the sons of Zebedee selfishly grasped for prominent places of leadership in Jesus' messianic kingdom, He pointed to His death as the decisive sign that leadership in His kingdom must take the form of servanthood: "For the Son of man also came not to be served but to serve, and to give his life as a ransom for many" (Mark 10:45).[25] He expected to die in the place of others—a conviction unforgettably enunciated at the Last Supper. At this momentous occasion Jesus explained to His disciples in words that were carefully preserved and handed down in oral tradition in the early church that His coming death was a vicarious death for the sake of others. All four versions of the Eucharistic words (except perhaps Luke where the text is uncertain) preserve this central notion. "This is my body which is for you" (1 Corinthians 11:24). "This is my blood of the covenant, which is poured out for many for the forgiveness of sins" (Matthew 26:28). Jesus saw His death as a sacrificial inaugural of a new covenant. As Cranfield says in the *Cambridge Greek Testament Commentary:* "As the Old Covenant had been ratified by the sprinkling of sacrificial blood (Exodus 24:6-8), so God's New Covenant with men is about to be established by Jesus' death."[26]

That the cross is the ultimate demonstration that God deals with His enemies through suffering love receives its clearest theological expression in Paul. "God shows his love for us in that while we were yet sinners, Christ died for us. . . . While we were enemies we were reconciled to God by the death of his Son" (Romans 5:8, 10). Jesus' vicarious cross for sinners is the foundation and deepest expression of Jesus' command to love one's enemies. We are enemies in the double sense both that sinful persons are hostile to God and also that the just, holy Creator hates sin (Romans 1:18). For those who know the law, failure to obey it results in a divine curse. But Christ redeemed us from that curse by becoming a curse for us (Galatians 3:10-14). Jesus' blood on the cross was an expiation (Romans 5:18) for us sinful enemies of God because the One who knew no sin was made sin for us on the cross (2 Corinthians 5:21).

Jesus' vicarious death for sinful enemies of God lies at

the very heart of our commitment to nonviolence. It was because the incarnate One knew that God was loving and merciful even toward the worst of sinners that He associated with sinners, forgave their sins, and completed His mission of dying for the sins of the world. And it was precisely the same understanding of God that prompted Him to command His followers to love their enemies. It is because we as God's children are to imitate the loving characteristics of our heavenly Father who mercifully showers His sun and rain on the just and unjust that we are to love our enemies. And the vicarious cross of Christ is the fullest expression of this aspect of God's nature. For at the cross, God Himself suffers for sinners in the person of His incarnate Son. Certainly we can never fathom all the mystery there. But it is precisely because the One hanging limp on the cross was the Word who became flesh that we know for sure both that a just God mercifully accepts us sinful enemies and also that He wants us to go and treat all our enemies in the same merciful, self-sacrificial way.

Because Jesus commanded His followers to love their enemies and then died as the incarnate Son to demonstrate that God reconciles His enemies by suffering love, any rejection of the nonviolent way in human relations involves a heretical doctrine of the atonement.[27] If God in Christ reconciled His enemies by suffering servanthood, then those who want to follow Christ faithfully dare not treat their enemies in any other way.

It is a tragedy of our time that many of those who appropriate the biblical understanding of Christ's vicarious cross fail to see its direct implications for the problem of war and violence. And it is equally tragic that some of those who most emphasize pacifism and nonviolence fail to ground it in Christ's vicarious atonement. It is a serious heresy of the atonement to base one's nonviolence in the weak sentimentality of the lowly Nazarene viewed merely as a noble martyr to truth and peace rather than in the vicarious cross of the Word who became flesh. The cross is much more than "Christ's witness to the weakness and folly of the sword"[28] although it certainly is that. In fact, it is that precisely because the incarnate Word's vicarious death for our sins is the ultimate demonstration that the Sovereign of the universe is a merciful Father who reconciles His enemies through self-sacrificial love.

Given this understanding of Jesus as the unique Son of God and His cross as the demonstration of God's method of dealing with enemies, it is hardly surprising that the New Testament writers regularly urged Christians to pattern their lives after Jesus' cross. Certainly the once-for-all sacrifice of Christ for the sins of the world was a unique element of His cross that could never be repeated.[29] But that fact never prevented the New Testament authors from discerning in the cross a decisive ethical clue for the Christian's approach to opponents and enemies, indeed even friends, spouses, and fellow members of Christ's body.

The recipients of the Epistle to the Ephesians lived in a male-dominated Hellenistic society. But that did not deter the author from urging husbands to treat their wives with the same self-sacrificing love that Jesus incarnated at the cross. "Husbands, love your wives, as Christ loved the church and gave himself up for her" (Ephesians 5:25). What pervasive quiet agony, what widespread aching unfulfillment would be avoided if Christian husbands followed the way of the cross in their homes. The way of the cross is not merely the exciting nonviolent stance that Gandhi and Martin Luther King used so successfully to change history. It is also God's way to peace and fulfillment in the difficult, doggedly persistent struggles that trouble every husband and wife from time to time.

In similar fashion, Philippians 2 holds up the cross as the clue to accord and harmony in the church. Paul introduces the marvelous hymn (vv. 6 ff.) about Jesus' self-emptying, His taking the form of a slave, and His obeying even to the extent of death on the cross to illustrate the kind of humility and unselfish concern for others that Christians ought to show toward each other (vv. 1-5). "The attitude you should have is one that Christ Jesus had" (v. 5, TEV). This Pauline injunction corresponds perfectly to Jesus' teaching that leadership in His kingdom would be via servanthood rather than oppression (Luke 22:24-27). What an incredible amount of division and scandal would have been prevented in the history of the church if Christians had followed Paul's admonition to pattern their relationships with sisters and brothers after the model of Christ's cross.

But the cross as model for human relationships is not limited to family and church in the epistles anymore than it is in Jesus. We saw earlier that Jesus commanded His followers to adopt the revolutionary stance of love for enemies in public areas such as the legal system and relationships with political oppressors. The epistles do the same.

The famous passage on government in Romans 13 is framed by a vigorous Pauline statement which, although it does not explicitly refer to the cross, clearly echoes Jesus' command to love one's enemies:

> Bless those who persecute you; bless and do not curse
> them. . . . Repay no one evil for evil. . . . Beloved, never
> avenge yourselves, but leave it to the wrath of God. . . . No,
> "if your enemy is hungry, feed him. . . ." Do not be over-
> come by evil, but overcome evil with good (Romans 12:14-
> 21).

Then after dealing with the topic of submission to
governmental authorities, Paul returns to the theme of
love for neighbor and insists that "love does no wrong to
a neighbor" (12:10). Whatever submission to government may mean—and we will examine that question in
some depth in chapter two—it surely does not mean par-
ticipating in lethal governmental violence, for Paul had
just insisted that the way of love meant forsaking
vengeance and loving one's enemies. Thus the way of the
cross also applies to the Christian's relationships with
government.

Finally, in 1 Peter 2 the appeal is for oppressed slaves
who have become Christians to submit not only to kind
owners but also to cruel masters.

> For one is approved if, mindful of God, he endures pain
> while suffering unjustly. . . . For to this you have been
> called, because Christ also suffered for you, leaving you an
> example, that you should follow in his steps. He committed
> no sin; no guile was found on his lips. When he was reviled,
> he did not revile in return; when he suffered, he did not
> threaten; but he trusted to him who judges justly. He
> himself bore our sins in his body on the tree, that we might
> die to sin and live to righteousness. By his wounds you have
> been healed (1 Peter 2:19-24).

It is as one is mindful of the nature of God which was

revealed most fully in Jesus' cross that one can endure
even unjustly inflicted suffering. With direct references
to the Suffering Servant of Isaiah 53, 1 Peter explicitly
commands Christians to imitate Jesus on the cross when
they confront unjust oppressors. I do not think that
means that oppressed slaves or contemporary victims of
systemic injustice must passively acquiesce in their oppression. But it does mean that if they obey the biblical
command to follow Christ's example, they will refuse to
regard oppressors as enemies to be reviled and hated.
Rather, precisely as they remember that Christ died for
their sins while they were still enemies of God, they will
imitate God's unfathomable love for enemies incarnated
in His Son's cross.

In every strand of New Testament literature and with
reference to every kind of situation (whether family,
church, state, or employment), the way of the cross applies. Jesus' cross, where He practiced what He had
preached about love for one's enemies, becomes the
Christian norm for every area of life. Only if one holds
biblical authority so irrelevant that one can ignore explicit, regularly repeated scriptural teaching; only if one
so disregards Christ's atonement that one rejects God's
way of dealing with enemies; only then can one forsake
the cross for the sword.

To be sure, church history is a sad story of Christians
doing precisely that. After the first three centuries when
almost all Christians refused to participate in warfare,[30]
Christians repeatedly invented ways to justify violence.

And each of us if we think honestly about the costly
implications of suffering servanthood, will understand
within ourselves how temptingly plausible it is to
consider Jesus' nonviolent way an impossible ideal, a

utopian vision practiced only in the millennium, or some idealistic teaching intended only for personal relationships. But if one recalls Jesus' historical context, one simply cannot assert that that is what Jesus Himself meant. Claiming to be their Messiah, He came to an oppressed people ready to use violence to drive out their oppressors. But He advocated love for enemies as God's method for ushering in the coming kingdom. And He submitted to Roman crucifixion to reconcile His enemies.

If, as unbelievers of both past and present assert, the cross is the last word about Jesus of Nazareth, then His call to suffering servanthood was indeed a noble but ultimately utopian dream that responsible realists should ignore. But if as Christians claim, the grave could not hold Him, then His messianic kingdom has truly begun and the way of the cross is the way of the Risen Sovereign of this whole glorious universe.

Lord, I believe, help Thou my unbelief. Amen.

Discussion Questions

1. What were the political options that Jesus faced?
2. How similiar to and how different from our world today was the world of Jesus?
3. Why was Jesus crucified?
4. What reasons are there for thinking that Jesus' command to love one's enemies applies in public as well as private life?
5. How is the way of the cross rooted in the nature of God?
6. Do you think that the way of the cross can be applied today in our modern world in all the areas in which the epistles apply it?

2
Christ and Power

Christ and Power

What does the cross have to do with power? Can a follower of the Suffering Servant use some forms of force and coercion in a nonviolent search for justice? Or are we to adopt a genuinely nonresistant stance in the face of evil? Should we opt for an activist nonviolence or a quietist nonresistance?

The nonresistant person believes that the Sermon on the Mount precludes the Christian's use not just of lethal physical violence but also institutional force such as codes of behavior and laws with threats of punishment.[1] The death principle is at work not only when a factory owner exploits his workers, but also "when a community tries to impose its standards of morality with the penalty of law."[2] It is crucial, of course, to understand that this nonresistant stance is by no means apolitical merely because it rejects the economic power of boycotts and the political pressure of organized lobbying. Merely living out the full reality of Jesus' new community where the Old Age's dividing walls of race, class, sex, and nation have been transcended is a powerful political statement. Simply announcing the full biblical word about sin, which has institutional as well as personal forms, is profoundly political. At times nonresistance has degenerated into silent support for an unjust status quo. But when that has happened, nonresistance has been unfaithful to its own best insight. Nonresistance is not apolitical even though it rejects the use of economic and political force as acceptable means for social change.

But is nonresistance really the way of the Man from Nazareth? I want to argue in this chapter that the use of economic and political power may be, indeed is, fully compatible with the way of the cross as outlined in chapter one. I think activist nonviolence rather than nonresistance is the more faithful application of New Testament teaching. The Historic Peace Churches lack an adequate theology of power. In this chapter I want to attempt to reflect on what forms of power are compatible with the way of suffering servanthood.

Power, according to Weber's celebrated definition, "is the probability that one actor within a social relationship will be in a position to carry out his [or her!] own will despite resistance, regardless of the basis on which this probability rests."[3] If that is what power is, then clearly even nonresistant Christians think some forms of it are quite permissible. We use parental power—quite properly I would argue—to enforce certain minimal standards of cleanliness, civility, and cooperation in the home. That involves power. We use both sociological and religious power when we exercise church discipline in the believers' church and finally as a last resort reluctantly excommunicate those who persistently resist the counsel of sisters and brothers.

There are many kinds of force or coercion. Force is present when a parent disciplines a child. It is present in every social setting. It is present in economics and politics. And, of course, it is present in a lethal way in war.

I believe that one can distinguish between forms of coercion which love and respect the other person as a free moral agent responsible to the Creator and forms of coercion that do not. It is possible to use psychological, sociological, or economic coercion in a way that respects and preserves the other person's freedom to persist in saying "No." A law with legal penalties does that because the person can decide to disobey and accept the penalty. An economic boycott does that because the person can choose to suffer the economic consequences. A consciously constructed Christian community also does that even though (as the sociologist rightly points out) enormous coercive power is at work. One can engage in all the above forms of genuine coercion and still lovingly appeal *at the same time* to the other person as a free moral agent responsible to God to choose to repent and change.

Lethal violence is different. When one kills another person, one treats him as a thing, not a person. Hence Jesus' teaching excludes lethal violence as an acceptable option for Christians.

Love must also be the goal or end of acceptable forms of coercion. An economic boycott to end oppression has the loving aim of liberation and justice for the oppressor as well as the oppressed. And, as we just noted, it can be conducted in such a way that one genuinely loves the other person and respects his freedom as a person responsible to God. For coercion to be acceptable, then, love must be both the means and the end. It is undoubtedly wrong to use power over others simply because of a desire to coerce and dominate.[4] But it is not wrong to use nonlethal forms of coercion if the end and means are love for all parties.

But how does all this square with Jesus and the rest of the New Testament? Does a New Testament understanding of power enable one to distinguish acceptable and nonacceptable forms of power?

I want to begin with Jesus.[5] Does not Jesus' clear command, "Do not resist one who is evil," flatly contradict the kind of activist nonviolence just outlined? Does Jesus' command not preclude the use of economic and political power to oppose unjust, evil persons and structures? Some have thought so and argued that Jesus' followers dare not use force of any kind to resist evil. But to interpret Matthew 5:39 in that way is surely to prove too much. If we are to interpret it literally, then we must consistently apply it in a literal fashion in every area. If the text calls for literal nonresistance, then that means absolute nonresistance toward evil persons in the home and in the congregation just as much as in the search for justice in the marketplace or in the political arena. It simply will not do to apply the text literally in some areas and conclude that Jesus' nonresistance forbids boycotts and strikes and then apply the text in a nonliteral fashion in the home and in the congregation. Either Matthew 5:39 demands absolute nonresistance toward evil in every area or we dare not interpret it absolutely literally in any area.

Numerous actions in the life of Jesus would seem to support the latter alternative. Jesus constantly opposed evil persons in a forthright, vigorous fashion. He unleashed a blistering attack on the Pharisees. Denouncing them as blind guides, fools, hypocrites, and a brood of vipers, He uttered a harsh public condemnation of their many errors, including their preoccupation with tithing on small matters and their neglect of more important things like justice and mercy (Matthew 23:13-33).

Nor was Jesus nonresistant when He cleansed the temple! He engaged in aggressive resistance against evil when He marched into the temple, drove the animals out with a whip, dumped the money tables upside down, and denounced the money changers as robbers. If Matthew 5:39 means that all forms of resistance to evil are forbidden, then Jesus contradicted His own teaching. Jesus certainly did not kill the money changers. Indeed, I doubt that He even used His whip on them. But He certainly resisted their evil in a dramatic act of civil disobedience.

Or consider Jesus' response when a soldier unjustly struck Him on the cheek at His trial (John 18:19-24). Instead of turning the other cheek and meekly submitting to this injustice, He protested! "If I have spoken wrongly, bear witness to the wrong; but if I have spoken rightly, why do you strike me?" Apparently Jesus thought that protesting police brutality or engaging in civil disobedience in a nonviolent fashion was entirely consistent with His command not to resist one who is evil.

What then does Matthew 5:39 mean? It means two very radical things: (1) that one should not resist evil persons by exacting equal damages for injury suffered (i.e., an eye for an eye); and (2) that one should not respond to an evil person by placing him in the category of enemy. Indeed, one should love one's enemies, even at great personal cost. The good of the other person, not one's own needs or rights, are decisive.

Jesus' command not to resist evil must be understood in light of the preceding verse. To exact an eye for an eye was the accepted norm. But Jesus rejected that way of dealing with evil persons. One should not resist evil in that way. The Greek preposition ἀντί (which means "opposite" or "instead of" or "in place of") appears in both verses. It appears in the phrase an eye for (ἀντί) an eye and a tooth for (ἀντί) a tooth. Then it appears in the verb resist (ἀντιστῆναι). Literally ἀντιστῆναι means "to stand opposite" or "to place against." The repetition of the preposition in both verses suggests that one is not to place oneself against an evil person in the way indicated in verse 38, which was the normally accepted way—i.e., by exacting equal damages for injury suffered. In fact, one is to respond to evil by refusing to place the person who inflicts evil in the category of an enemy to be hated or injured. Instead of categorizing the person who harms one as an enemy, one is to love him. And that love is to be so clear and costly and so singlemindedly focused on the needs of the other person that it will even accept additional insult and injury from the wicked person. One should respond with that kind of astonishing, unexpected love for the evil person even when he strikes one's right cheek with the back of his hand, which was considered the most insulting of all physical blows.[6] But that does not mean that we cannot offer any form of resistance to the evil person. That would contradict Jesus' own rebuke of the soldier who struck Him on the cheek. Rather it means that Jesus' kind of resistance to evil will be of the sort that refuses to exact equal damages for injury suffered, that refuses to consider anyone an enemy no matter how outrageous his offense and therefore that continues to demonstrate active aggressive love controlled by the need of the evil person. Thus Jesus' saying is compatible with the use of economic, legal, or political power to oppose evil as long as love for the oppressor as well as the oppressed is both the means and the end.

One hypothetical illustration might help. Suppose one were a businessperson with a client who refused to repay $30,000. Would it be legitimate to sue him in court and thus apply legal force? Well, it all depends. Certainly not if he were a fellow Christian. In that case, as Paul indicates, we should lay it before the other sisters and brothers and accept their decision. But what if the person is not a Christian? Could you then sue him? Not necessarily. The good of the other person is the decisive consideration. If the other party cannot repay the money, then you should suffer financial loss to demonstrate your love. On the other hand, if you decided after much prayer and group discernment that the other party could pay but was merely trying to avoid his proper responsibilities, then it would be in the interest of the other person to take him to court.

We have looked at Jesus to see if the use of power is compatible with His life and teaching. Next, I want to examine the Pauline concept of the principalities and powers to see if that will give us further insight about the Christian attitude toward power. In his chapter on the principalities and powers in *The Politics of Jesus*, John Howard Yoder makes the following statement on which, I hope, he will sometime elaborate at length:

But if the disciple of Jesus Christ chooses not to exercise certain kinds of power, this is not simply because they are powerful; for the Powers as such, power in itself, is the good creation of God. He chooses not to exercise certain types of power because, in a given context, the rebellion of the structure of a given particular power is so incorrigible that at the time the most effective way to *take* responsibility is to refuse to collaborate, and by that refusal to take sides in favor of the man whom that power is oppressing. ... The church must be sufficiently experienced to be able to discern when and where and how God is using the Powers, whether this be thanks to the faithful testimony of the church or in spite of her infidelity. Either way, she is called to contribute to the creation of structures more worthy of man.[7]

What does the Pauline doctrine of the Powers tell us about whether the nonviolent Christian should use power to create more just social structures?

There is growing agreement that when Paul speaks of the principalities and powers (ἀρχαί καί ἐξουσίαι) he refers to *both* the sociopolitical structures of human society *and* to unseen spiritual forces that undergird, lie behind, and in some mysterious way help shape human sociopolitical structures.[8] That the principalities and powers are not merely superhuman spiritual beings is quite clear in Colossians 2:8-23 where the principalities and powers that Christ disarmed include things like philosophy, *human* traditions (v. 8), and religious regulations about dietary laws and Sabbath observance. That the principalities and powers are not, on the other hand, merely sociopolitical structures of human society is also clear. Ephesians 6:12 says that we contend not "against flesh and blood, but against the principalities, against the powers, against the world rulers of this present darkness, against the spiritual hosts of wickedness in the heavenly places."[9]

In his book, *The Powers That Be*,[10] Clinton Morrison has clarified this Pauline conception. C. E. B. Cranfield summarizes Morrison's important contribution: "He has shown with a wealth of evidence that 'there was a common Graeco-Roman concept of the State,' according to which rulers were 'divinely appointed in relation to a cosmic system of spiritual powers,' and he has gone a long way towards proving that this was a conception shared alike by the Graeco-Roman world, Hellenistic Jews, and early Christians, and that therefore the fact that nowhere in the New Testament is this relationship between civil rulers and spiritual powers explicitly affirmed is no reason for doubting that it is assumed."[11] Some may doubt that a scientific age can accept such a notion of extra-empirical reality. But I confess that as I ponder the pervasive character and terrifying power of the forces of evil both in myself and in contemporary social structures, I have no trouble accepting the Pauline view. For Paul, in any case, the words "principalities and powers" connote both the empirically visible sociopolitical structures of our world and also invisible spiritual forces that help shape those visible structures.

In spite of the pervasive evil that he perceived in the principalities and powers, Paul insisted that they were not innately evil. The principalities and powers are a part of the good creation: "For in him [Christ] all things were created, in heaven and on earth, visible and invisible, whether thrones or dominions or *principalities or authorities* [powers]—all things were created through him and for him" (Colossians 1:16). If the principalities and powers are part of the good creation, it would seem to follow that power itself is not evil. It is only when power is used for an evil purpose or when the methods used are

not compatible with the methods of Jesus' kingdom that
the Christian must say no to power.

The Pauline view that the principalities and powers
are part of the good creation would seem to support the
view that government is not merely a necessity because
of the Fall. Rather, government is necessary and desira-
ble for human existence, not just fallen human existence.[12]

The expectation that the principalities and powers will
ultimately be purged of the corrupting effects of the Fall
underlines Paul's view that they are part of the good
creation. After noting in Colossians 1:16 that all things
both visible and invisible in heaven and earth were
created through Jesus Christ, Paul goes on to declare that
"all things, whether on earth or in heaven" will finally be
reconciled to God through the cross (v. 20). The phrase
"whether on earth or in heaven" surely includes an explicit reference to the principalities and powers. At the
final consummation then, when the good creation is
purged of all the ghastly corruption of the Fall, the sinful
principalities and powers will also be reconciled to the
Creator against whom they rebelled.

But immediately an objection appears. Does not 1
Corinthians suggest that the principalities and powers
will be destroyed rather than restored? According to the
Revised Standard Version, 1 Corinthians 2:6 says that the
rulers of this age are "doomed to pass away." And 1
Corinthians 15:24 declares that Christ will deliver the
kingdom to God the Father "after destroying every rule
[ἀρχήν] and every authority [ἐξουσίαν] and power [δύνα-
μιν]." But is this the proper translation? The key word in
both passages is the verb καταργεῖν . This verb means
"to make ineffective or powerless." It also means "to

abolish or destroy." The latter meaning is clearly present in 1 Corinthians 15:26 where Paul says, "The last enemy to be destroyed [καταργεῖται] is death." Since this verse follows closely after verse 24 and is part of the argument about Christ's final victory, perhaps we should assume that Paul also thinks of the destruction of the principalities and powers in verse 24.[13]

But the verb does not always mean "destroy." In 1 Corinthians 13:8, Paul says that our present prophecies and knowledge are imperfect and will therefore pass away (καταργηθήσεται).[14] But he does not mean that knowledge will be destroyed; rather, he means that the imperfections of our present understanding will be removed. "Now I know in part; then I shall understand fully" (v. 12). Although our present knowledge is woefully inadequate, the Eschaton will not destroy it. Rather it transforms it by purging it of imperfections and inadequacies.

Perhaps the best way to understand Paul's meaning in 1 Corinthians 2:6 and 15:24 is to look at Colossians 2:15. This verse contains Paul's most explicit statement about what happened to the principalities and powers at the cross. Paul says Christ "disarmed the principalities and powers and made a public example of them, triumphing over them in him." Three key verbs stand out. The first one tells us that the principalities and powers have been disarmed. To disarm someone is not to destroy him. Rather it is to strip him of his power to do evil. The second verb in this sentence means to expose or make a public display of someone—e.g., to publicly disgrace an adulteress. The last verb is the most vivid of the three. Θριαμβεύσαι means to lead a triumphal procession. This verb refers to the practices of the Roman army. "When a

Roman general had subdued another nation, the rulers of
that nation had to march into Rome on their bare feet,
behind the chariot on which the conqueror rode."[15] The
principalities and powers were part of the good creation
but they rebelled against God. At the cross, Christ
stripped them of their power, made a public display of
their weakness, and forced them to follow humbly as
conquered enemies in His triumphal procession. But
again, nothing here suggests the destruction of the principalities and powers although it certainly indicates that
they are stripped of their power to do evil. Therefore
Paul goes right on to assert (Colossians 2:16-23) that
human traditions and religious customs need have no
power over Christians since Christ has already robbed
them—the principalities and powers!—of their power.

I conclude then that Paul does not mean to say in 1
Corinthians 2:6 and 15:24 that the principalities and
powers are ultimately destroyed. Rather he means that at
the final consummation, they will be rendered powerless
to do evil.[16] These rebellious powers will be fully disarmed and will submit to the One who created them.

The vision of the final consummation in the Book of
Revelation confirms the view that the principalities and
powers will finally be reconciled rather than destroyed.
No biblical writer stresses the fallen character of the state
more than the seer of the Apocalypse. But he also writes
that in the Eschaton, the kings of the earth shall bring
their glory into the New Jerusalem.

> The city has no need of sun or moon to shine upon it, for
> the glory of God is its light, and its lamp is the Lamb. By its
> light shall the nations walk; and the kings of the earth shall
> bring their glory into it, and its gates shall never be shut by

day—and there shall be no night there; they shall bring into
it the glory and the honor of the nations (Revelation 21:23-
26).

To be sure, the nations as we know them will have to be
mightily transformed, for nothing unclean dare enter the
Holy City (21:27). But that will certainly happen for the
tree of life stands in the midst of the New Jerusalem and
its leaves are for the healing of the nations (22:2).

This eschatological hope for the restoration of the
whole of creation including the principalities and powers
underlines the fact that the Christian dare not choose
between a creation ethic and a kingdom ethic. Certainly
the fallen order is so corrupted that we cannot now
derive ethical norms merely from a careful reading of the
created order. Epistemologically our ethic will be a
revealed ethic, a kingdom ethic. But ontologically it must
also be a creation ethic or we begin to slip toward Mani-
chaeism and forget that this fallen creation will ultimately be redeemed.

This brief analysis of the New Testament conception
of the principalities and powers confirms the thesis
developed in the first section on Jesus. Power itself is not
innately evil. It is part of the good creation. Hence it can
and should be used by Christians in loving nonviolent
ways in the search for justice.

But how aggressive should we be in our confrontation
with the fallen principalities and powers of the marketplace and the forum? Should we merely give our witness
and prepare to defend ourselves or should we take the offensive?

That we should do the former is generally agreed. Our
witness to the powers involves proclaiming and living

both the reality of the church and the lordship of Christ. Ephesians 3 makes it quite clear that Christians are to proclaim and demonstrate the mystery of the church to the principalities and powers (vv. 7-10). Precisely this incarnation of the new reality of the people of God will be a profound political act. In a fallen world where the powers have erected hostile dividing walls of class, race, sex, and age, merely living out the full reality of Jesus' new community where all relationships—whether psychological, economic, or social—are *now* being redeemed is a profoundly political witness.

Equally political is the proclamation that Jesus Christ is Lord. Ephesians 6:10-20 makes it clear that in the battle with the principalities and powers (v. 12), we are to fight with the gospel, with truth, and with the word of God. It is central to the biblical word that precisely the One whom the principalities and powers crucified (1 Corinthians 2:8) is now their Lord and Master. The risen Jesus is Lord of the world as well as the church. Every strand of New Testament literature boldly proclaims this message. "All authority in heaven and on earth has been given to me," the risen Jesus told His disciples (Matthew 28:18). In Colossians 2:10, Paul declares that Christ is the head of the principalities and powers. The resurrected Christ is "far above all rule and authority and power and dominion, and above every name that is named, not only in this age [i.e., certainly in this age!] but also in that which is to come" (Ephesians 1:21). First Peter also reminds us that angels, authorities and powers are now subject to Christ (3:22). Likewise the author of Hebrews declares that everything is put in subjection under Christ (2:8, 9). Nowhere is this stated more powerfully than in the Book of Revelation where it is repeatedly affirmed that the risen Jesus is now "ruler of kings on earth" (1:5). Even now He is King of kings and Lord of lords (19:16; 17:14).

To announce Christ's lordship to the principalities and powers is to tell governments that they are not sovereign. It is to tell them that whether or not they know or acknowledge it, they are subject to the risen Lord Jesus who summons them to do justice, to seek peace, to promote shalom on the earth. It is to tell governments that Jesus Christ, who is one with the Father, is on the side of the poor and that He is at work in history pulling down the rich because of their oppression and neglect of the poor and exalting the lowly.[17] Again it is clear that *merely* to witness in a biblical way to the principalities and powers is to engage in dangerous, subversive political activity.

But is that all we are to do? Is it correct to say that we should witness to the state and other principalities and powers but not take the offensive against them? I think not. I doubt that the absence of offensive weapons in Ephesians 6:10-20 means that we are merely to defend ourselves against the powers.[18] Everyone agrees that we are to witness boldly to the powers. But surely that is an offensive act, not a defensive one. One can take the offensive with words just a much as with actions. Ephesians 6 calls us to arm ourselves with the truth, with the gospel, and with the Word of God. The kinds of words we are summoned to speak to the powers surely involves taking the offensive unless one wrongly supposes that bold proclamation is merely a defensive approach.

To say that we are not to take the offensive against the powers is to ignore the whole thrust of God's action in history. In the incarnation, God Himself steps into history to join battle with the forces of evil. Jesus took the offensive and constantly battled with the demonic forces during His public ministry. He took the offensive both against the Pharisees and also against the Sadducees because of their economic exploitation in the temple. He continued His offensive against the principalities and powers when He disarmed them at the cross and led them as captives in His triumphal procession. As the body of Christ, we are to continue the mission of the incarnate One in the world today and that includes an ongoing offensive against the fallen principalities and powers, a vigorous, active use of power in the search for greater justice in society.

But again we must face an objection. Is this kind of vigorous offensive compatible with Romans 13? Does not Paul call Christians to a nonresistant attitude toward even tyrannical governments?[19] Again I think not. To speak of nonresistance is to overstate the Pauline demand. Certainly Romans 13 rejects rebellion, not just against a just government, but against any government. Instead we are to be subject to whatever government exists for us.

As Cranfield and Yoder so clearly demonstrate, however, "to be subject" is not at all the same as "to obey." Cranfield insists that we must take seriously the fact that the word Paul uses for "be subject" (ὑποτάσσεσθαι) is not one of the normal words for "obey."

There are, of course, three perfectly good verbs meaning "obey," all of which are used in the New Testament, namely πειθαρχειν, πείθεσθαι, and ὑπακούειν. The LXX evidence confirms the impression given by Liddell and Scott. Of the twenty-one occurrences of ὑποτάσσεσθαι ...

there only seems to be one in which the idea of obedience is clearly prominent (Theod. Dan. vi. 13). In the New Testament, ὑποτάσσεσθαι occurs thirty times. Sometimes the idea of obedience is clearly prominent (e.g., Romans 8:7), but in the majority of cases, while it may be included, it is not clear that it predominates. . . . But what does ὑποτάσσεσθαι mean when it is used, as here, to denote that which the Christian owes to the civil authority . . . ? It means surely recognizing that one is placed below it by God. . . . It will not be uncritical, not a blind obedience to the authority's every command; for the arbiter of what constitutes ὑπο-τάσσεσθαι in a particular situation is not the civil power but Christ.[20]

Neither Jesus nor the early church ever supposed that to be subject to government meant to obey its every command. Jesus and the apostles knew that whenever government commanded what was contrary to God's command, it must be disobeyed. "We must obey God rather than men" (Acts 5:29) was their working principle. But even in their refusal to obey, even in their civil disobedience, they continued to be subject to government. They did not rebel. They did not take up the sword to overthrow government. On the other hand, when government commanded things contrary to God's will they regularly refused to obey, and then accepted the penalty for their disobedience. When Paul says that we are not to resist the authorities, he does not mean that we are never to disobey. That would contradict the practice and teaching of Christ and the apostles that sometimes we must disobey government in order to obey God. He means that we are not to rebel against government and deny that it has authority over us.

I think we are called to the same kind of wholehearted

subjection to government today. But that in no way is incompatible with a vigorous nonviolent offensive against, indeed active resistance to, governmental injustice. We should resist the evils promoted or perpetuated by governments. We dare not rebel against government and cast off its authority. We can and should try to make our government—no matter how good or bad it is—more just. We dare not—however unjust it may be—try to destroy it. We can engage in political lobbying, voter power, economic boycott, political demonstration, civil disobedience, tax refusal, even total noncooperation and still be subject to our government. As long as the methods are those of loving nonviolence, as long as we refuse to consider the oppressor an enemy, as long as we submissively reject rebellion and instead respectfully accept the penalties that are imposed, we remain subject to government. Scripture commands us always to be subject to government. It does not command us to obey without condition. And wholehearted subjection to government is fully compatible with the most vigorous nonviolent resistance to governmental injustice because the goal is not rebellion but improvement of the government to which we are subject precisely as we resist.

This distinction between resistance and rebellion is by no means merely semantic. The person who resists, resists only the oppression or injustice and continues to accept the government's authority. Furthermore the one who resists respects the government and calls on the governing officials as free moral agents to change and end their rebellion against the shalom willed by their true Sovereign, the risen Lord, who is in fact King of kings and Lord of lords. On the other hand, the one who rebels denies that the government has any authority and abandons any hope that the unjust rulers can be anything other than enemies to be removed.

I have argued that the nonviolent Christian can and should sometimes use various kinds of economic and political power (including economic boycotts and civil disobedience) to make secular socioeconomic-political structures more just. Obviously a host of problems and loose ends remain which cannot be dealt with here. But I must face one final objection: "Neither Jesus nor the apostolic church engaged in economic boycotts or civil disobedience to challenge and correct social injustice in the Roman Empire. And neither should we." What can be said to this important objection?

I want very briefly to sketch one response. The political situation in first-century Palestine was vastly different from the political situation in North America, Europe, and many other parts of the world today. Roman emperors were dictators. There was no place for a friendly opposition or for the expression of political dissent. Subject populations like the Jews could collaborate, either eagerly as did the Sadducees or less enthusiastically as did the Pharisees, or they could rebel as did the Zealots and get crucified. Jesus, as we have seen, rightly rejected all these political options. After He had rejected all the unfaithful modes of political activity in His particular historical context, there was no other viable political stance tolerated by the ruling dictatorship other than that of building a new community based on different values. That is exactly what He did. Nor was that not apolitical. The same situation confronted the early church, of course, and they responded in the same way. Not every historical context permits political activity (governed by kingdom norms) directed toward

the creation of more just social structures in secular society. When the historical context does not permit that
kind of political activity, then obviously it is not an obli-
gation. But the fact that it is not done in one kind of historical setting surely does not suggest that it should not
be done in another. In a democratic society, political
activity designed to promote structural change is possible. Even in many contemporary settings far less free
than our own, the constitution theoretically provides for
freedom of speech and political activity. Hence it is
possible to appeal to the government to respect its own
principles. Jesus and the apostles incarnated a passionate
concern for the needs of the whole person in a way that
was possible in their historicopolitical context. We should
do the same in historically appropriate ways in our different historical setting.

I urge that we move forward creatively and boldly in
the exercise of economic and political power. We need to
become co-workers with the oppressed as they rightly
search for a more just distribution of power in our world.
For some that will mean persistent, uncompromising ad-
vocacy of the rights of the oppressed from within present
economic and political systems. For others it will mean
economic boycotts, demonstrations, civil disobedience
and the building of alternative institutions. For both
groups, it will mean ongoing prayer and dialogue to see
when conscientious objection, conscientious refusal to
participate in a given corporation, election, or office is
the only faithful, effective way to exercise power. We
dare never suppose that a more extensive exercise of economic and political power means that we must always
choose one of the world's currently available options.

Nor dare we suppose that more attention to the

exercise of economic and political power in secular society will mean less concern for the church. Precisely as we plunge deeper into the centers of power of secular society, we will need even more urgently to strengthen the church as a counterculture of Christians whose visible commitment to the radical values of Jesus' new kingdom is so uncompromising that the church's very existence represents a fundamental challenge to surrounding society. Unless we are based in that kind of kingdom counterculture, our movement into society will be useless because we will merely become one more empty echo of an unjust status quo. But that need not happen if we maintain the sharp biblical distinction between the church and the world and if our primary identity and allegiance remains with Jesus' new community of believers.

Power is not innately evil. It is part of the good creation. God's people should use it in obedience to their Lord for the sake of His oppressed poor. Serve the Lord. Serve the people.

Discussion Questions

1. What is the difference between nonresistance and nonviolence?
2. What forms of power do you in fact use in your life every day, week, and year?
3. What do you think Jesus meant by saying, "Do not resist one who is evil"?
4. What does the Apostle Paul mean by the "principalities and powers"? What does this teaching of Paul tell us about the use of power (economic, political, and the like) by Christians?
5. What happened to the principalities and powers at the cross and how should today's church relate to them?

3
Peacemaking and Economics

Peacemaking and Economics[1]

Probably few people reading this book will have killed another person. Many would choose going to jail rather than going to war. But joining the army is not the only way to participate in murder. Established economic structures can destroy people by the millions. Slavery did that. Child labor did that. Both were as legal as they were lethal. Legal structures can be violent. Therefore we must face a very painful question: Do we participate in economic structures that help destroy millions of people each year?

The story of the sugar we stir into our coffee or tea suggests an answer. The largest sugar mill in the world is in the Dominican Republic.[2] A U.S. based multinational corporation, Gulf and Western, bought that sugar plant and huge sugar plantations shortly after President Johnson sent the U.S. marines into the Dominican Republic in 1965 to protect U.S. investments there. In the last twenty years, the amount of land used for growing sugar cane has doubled. But almost all of that sugar goes for export to us and other rich nations. In the last twenty years, the per capita production of food, excluding sugar, in the Dominican Republic has *decreased*. Over 50 percent of the people in the Dominican Republic are starving or malnourished, and 50 percent of the children die before they reach the age of five largely because they do not have enough food.

Not even the Dominicans who work on the sugar plantations have profited. The sugar plantation workers earned less in real wages in 1978 than they did in 1968— in part because the Dominican government installed by U.S. marines has destroyed the cane cutters' labor union. The U.S. has invested more money per capita for police training in the Dominican Republic than in any other Latin American country. And those police have made widespread use of torture to suppress any opposition to the dictatorship which ruled for over a decade. Fortunately that government was replaced in 1978, thanks in part to President Carter's vigorous support of the results of an election which the armed forces wanted to annul. But that former government has made it possible for Gulf and Western to use a vast part of the country's best land to grow sugar for you and me at a handsome profit to the company.

Now who is responsible for the thousands of Dominican children who die each year of malnutrition? Just the top leaders at Gulf and Western? Just the Dominican Republic's elite who profit by cooperating with Gulf and Western? Or are you and I also implicated?

Jacques Ellul has pointed out that unjust economic systems can be as violent as rampaging armies: "I maintain that all kinds of violence are the same . . . the violence of the soldier who kills, the revolutionary who assassinates; it is true also of economic violence—the violence of the privileged proprietor against his workers, of the 'haves' against the 'have-nots'; the violence done in international economic relations between our societies and those of the third world; the violence done through powerful corporations which exploit the resources of a country that is unable to defend itself."[3] One can only agree with James Douglass:

> In the contemporary world of affluence and poverty, where man's major crime is murder by privilege, revolution against the established order is the criterion of a living faith. ... Truly I say to you, as you did it not to one of the least of these, you did it not to me (Matt. 25:45). The murder of Christ continues. Great societies build on dying men.[4]

In the last 50 years, especially the last 20, the Brethren in Christ, the Church of the Brethren, and the Mennonites have moved more and more into the economic mainstream of our society. Therefore, if we look carefully at present economic structures, we are forced to the conclusion that we are involved in murder by privilege. Unfortunately it is not true that our society's wealth is simply the result of God's blessing and hard work. To a significant extent, our affluence depends on unjust economic structures that make us rich and Latin Americans hungry. Fully *one half* of all the cultivable land in Central America is used to grow export crops (sugar, coffee, bananas, flowers, and the like) to sell to the U.S., Canada, and other rich nations. That land ought to be used to grow food for the masses in Central America where 60 percent of the children die of malnutrition before they are five years old. But it is used to grow sugar and coffee and bananas for North Americans because we can pay for it and the starving children's parents cannot.

By the economic lifestyles we adopt, the economic structures that support those lifestyles and the politicians we elect (either by our votes or nonparticipation) to protect those structures, we participate in murder by privilege.

For Historic Peace Churches, that is a very painful situation to face. But if we are serious about our heritage of peacemaking, then we must explore more carefully than we have thus far how economic systems kill people just as surely as do guns and bombs.

I will explore the problem of institutionalized violence or structural sin in three steps. First, what is the biblical teaching on institutionalized violence? Second, how are we involved in it today? And third, what can we do about it?

There is an important difference between consciously willed, individual acts (like lying to a friend or committing an act of adultery) and participation in evil social structures. Slavery is an example of the latter. So is the Victorian factory system where ten-year-old children worked twelve to sixteen hours a day. Although both slavery and child labor were legal, they destroyed people by the millions. They represent institutionalized violence or structural evil. Tragically, most Christians seem to be more concerned with individual sinful acts than with participation in violent social structures.

But the Bible condemns both. Speaking through His prophet Amos, the Lord declared,

For three transgressions of Israel, and for four, I will not revoke the punishment; because they sell the righteous for silver, and the needy for a pair of shoes—they that trample the head of the poor into the dust of the earth, and turn aside the way of the afflicted; a man and his father go in to the same maiden, so that my holy name is profaned (Amos 2:6, 7).

Biblical scholars have shown that some kind of legal fiction underlies the phrase "selling the needy for a pair of shoes." This mistreatment of the poor was *legal!* In one breath God condemns both adultery and legalized oppression of the poor. Sexual sins and economic injustice are equally displeasing to God.

Some young activists have supposed that as long as they were fighting for the rights of minorities and opposing militarism, they were morally righteous regardless of how often they shacked up for the night with a guy or a girl in the movement. Some of their elders, on the other hand have supposed that because they did not lie, steal, and fornicate, they were morally upright even though they lived in segregated communities and owned stock in companies that exploit the poor of the earth. God, however, has shown that robbing one's workers of a fair wage is just as sinful as robbing a bank.

God clearly revealed that laws themselves are sometimes an abomination to him.

Can wicked rulers be allied with thee, who frame mischief by statute? They band together against the life of the righteous, and condemn the innocent to death. But the Lord has become my stronghold, and my God the rock of my refuge. He will bring back on them their iniquity and wipe them out for their wickedness; the Lord our God will wipe them out (Psalm 94:20-23).

The Jerusalem Bible translates verse 20 this way: "You never consent to that corrupt tribunal that imposes disorder as law." God wants us to know that wicked governments "frame mischief by statute." Or, as *The New English* Bible puts it, they contrive evil "under cover of law."

God proclaims the same word through the prophet Isaiah:

> Woe to those who decree iniquitous decrees, and the writers who keep writing oppression, to turn aside the needy from justice and to rob the poor of my people of their right . . . (Isaiah 10:1-4).

It is quite possible to make oppression legal. But legalized oppression is an abomination to our God. Therefore, He commands His people to oppose it.

There is one other aspect to institutionalized violence or structural evil which makes it especially pernicious. It is so subtle that one can be ensnared almost without realizing it.

God inspired His prophet Amos to utter some of the harshest words in Scripture against the cultured, kind, upper-class women of his day:

> Hear this word, you cows of Bashan . . . [you] who oppress the poor, who curse the needy, who say to . . . [your] husbands, "Bring, that we may drink!" The Lord God has sworn by his holiness that, behold, the days are coming upon you, when they shall take you away with hooks, even the last of you with fishhooks (Amos 4:1, 2).

The women involved probably had no contact with the

impoverished peasants. They may never have realized clearly that their gorgeous clothes and spirited parties were possible only because of the sweat and tears of toiling peasants. In fact, they may even have been kind to individual peasants they met. (Perhaps they gave them "Christmas baskets"—once a year.) But God called these privileged women cows because they profited from structural evil. Hence they were personally and individually guilty before God.

We must conclude, I think, that if we are members of a privileged class that profits from structural violence and if we do nothing to try to change things, then we stand guilty before God. Structural evil is just as sinful as personal evil. And it hurts more people and is more subtle.

With this biblical teaching on structural evil or institutionalized violence in mind, we can now ask the second question: Are we involved in structural violence today? Three areas deserve attention: international trade, our consumption of nonrenewable natural resources, and our eating patterns.

First, the patterns of international trade. The industrialized nations have carefully shaped the patterns of international trade for their own economic advantage. Tariff and other import restrictions are one part of the injustice in international trade. The United States charges the highest tariffs on processed and manufactured goods from poor countries. The less manufacturing and processing done by the poor country, the lower the tariff. The reason is simple. Entrenched processing and manufacturing interests (both labor and management) want the United States to be able to buy cheap raw materials and profit from processing and manufacturing them here. The result, unfortunately, is to deprive poor countries of millions of extra jobs and billions of extra dollars from increased exports.

Second and even more serious is the fact that for decades the prices of primary products sold by developing nations have been declining relative to the prices of manufactured products and other high technology items which poor countries must buy from developed nations. The following examples illustrate the effect.

The government of Tanzania reports that one tractor cost 5 tons of sisal in 1963. In 1970 the same tractor cost 10 tons of sisal. In 1960 a rubber exporting country could purchase six tractors with 25 tons of rubber. In 1975 the same amount of rubber would only buy two tractors. One could present many more examples that the present patterns of international trade are fundamentally unjust.

Second, we are involved in structural violence in our consumption of nonrenewable natural resources. Is it just for 5 percent of the world's people living in the United States to consume approximately 33 percent of the world's limited, nonrenewable energy and minerals each year?

Third, our eating patterns. At first glance our eating patterns may seem very personal and private. But they are tightly interlocked with complex economic structures—national and international agricultural policies and decisions of multinational corporations engaged in agribusiness.

The rich nations import far more food from poor nations than they export to them. Poor developing nations are feeding the affluent minority! Astonishingly, since 1955, every year the rich, developed nations imported approximately twice as many dollars' worth of food from poor, developing nations as they exported to them.

But what about us? Well the U.S. exports more than it imports. But the situation looks startlingly different when one examines only U.S. food imports from and exports to poor, developing nations. Every year the United States imports more food from poor nations than it exports to hungry lands!

The United States imports about twice as much fish (most of it primarily for feed for livestock) as do all the poor countries combined. Two thirds of the total world catch of tuna comes to the United States—and we feed one third of that to our cats.

Cowboys and beef cattle are part of our national self-identity. Surely our beef at least is all grown at home. By no means! The United States is the world's largest importer of beef! Imported beef comes not just from Australia and New Zealand, but also from many countries in Latin America, where at least 40 percent of the people are seriously malnourished. Nor is the problem merely that we consume beef that hungry Latin American children need. Our demand for beef also encourages unjust structures in Latin America.

Take the example of Honduras. Honduras is a poor Central American country where one third of the people earn less than thirty dollars a year. In spite of widespread poverty they export some 34.8 million pounds of beef to the United States each year. Beef for export is grown largely by a tiny wealthy elite of 667 families (.3 percent of the total population) who own 27.4 percent of all cultivable land.

In the last few years an intense struggle has raged in Honduras. The poor peasants want more land while predictably the powerful Honduran Cattle Farmers' Federation, which represents the wealthy farmers, objects. The wealthy farmers want to continue growing beef for Americans.

The infant mortality rate in Honduras is six times that of the United States. The World Bank indicates that malnutrition is either the primary cause or a major contributor to the death of 50-75 percent of all one-to-four-year-old children who die in Latin America. Who is responsible for those dying children? The wealthy Hondurans who want to protect their affluence? The American companies and the U.S. government that work closely with the Honduran elite? We who eat the beef needed by hundreds of thousands of hungry children in Honduras?

We dare not, of course, make the simplistic assumption that if we merely stop eating beef, hungry Hondurans will promptly enjoy it. Complex economic and political changes are required. The point here is that our eating patterns are interlocked with destructive social and economic structures that leave millions hungry and starving.

We are all implicated in structural evil. The patterns of international trade are unjust. An affluent minority devours most of the earth's nonrenewable natural resources. And the food consumption patterns in the world are grossly lopsided. Every North American benefits from these structural injustices. Unless you have retreated to some isolated valley and grow or make everything you use, you participate in unjust structures which contribute directly to the hunger of a billion unhappy neighbors.

But that is not God's last word to us. If there were no hope of forgiveness, admission of our complicity in guilt of this magnitude would be an act of despair. But there is hope—if we repent.

Thus far I have analyzed the problem and suggested that we need to repent of our sinful involvement in the institutionalized violence in our international economic order. But biblical repentance is not just a liturgical confession or a hasty fear. It is a whole new outlook and a radically new way of living. How then should we change?

We need change at three levels: (1) our personal lifestyles, (2) the church, and (3) secular society. In each case, the goal is peacemaking. More simple personal lifestyles will help us consume a less unfair share of the world's resources. More simple personal lifestyles will also free up time and resources to help end hunger and injustice in the world. Dramatic new forms of sharing in the one worldwide body of Christ would provide a new model for our global village dangerously divided between rich and poor. And structural change that would eliminate some of the systemic causes of hunger and poverty would also improve the chances of peace in our world. Senator Mark Hatfield has said: "The greatest threat to the stability of the entire world is hunger. It's more explosive than all the atomic weaponry possessed by the big powers. Desperate people do desperate things." If he is correct, then peacemaking through economic change in ourselves, the church, and secular society is one of the most pressing tasks today. Three areas call for attention.

First we need to pursue simpler personal lifestyles. As the Catholic saint, Elizabeth Seton, has said, "The rich must live more simply that the poor may simply live." But that is very hard in our consumer-oriented materialistic society. We have been enticed by unprecedented material luxury. Advertising constantly convinces us that we really need one unnecessary luxury after another.

The standard of living is the god of twentieth-century America, and the ad man is its prophet. We Christians need to make some dramatic, concrete moves to escape the materialism that seeps into our minds via the diabolically clever and incessant radio and television commercials.

The graduated tithe is one very modest proposal which can help break this materialistic stranglehold. I share it because it has proved helpful in our family.

When Arbutus and I decided to adopt a graduated scale for our giving in 1969, we started by sitting down and trying to calculate honestly what we would need to live for a year. We wanted a figure that would permit reasonable comfort but not all the luxuries. Somehow we arrived at a figure of $7,000. (Two growing boys and a new daughter have recently raised it to $8,000.) We decided to continue giving a tithe of 10 percent on this basic amount. Then for every additional thousand dollars of income above that basic amount, we decided to increase our giving by 5 percent on that $1000.

The graduated tithe is only one model. There are many others such as communal living and living at the level of welfare recipients. They all raise tough theoretical questions and even tougher practical questions when you try to implement them. But the basic question is really whether we will dare to measure our lifestyles by the needs of the poor rather than by the practices of our affluent neighbors.

My second set of proposals pertains to the church. I want to suggest two theses: (1) without new forms which help us recapture the early church's powerful experience of community in Christ's body, it will be impossible to implement biblical teaching on our relationship toward the poor; and (2) it is a farce to ask Washington to legislate what the church refuses to live.

The church should consist of communities of loving defiance. Instead it consists largely of comfortable clubs of conformity. A far-reaching reformation of the church is a prerequisite if the church today is to commit itself to Jesus' mission of liberating the oppressed.

The God of the Bible is calling Christians today to live in fundamental nonconformity to contemporary society. Affluent North American society is obsessed with materialism, sex, economic success, and military might. Things are more important than persons. Job security and an annual salary increase matter more than starving children and oppressed peasants. Paul's warning to the Romans is especially pertinent today: "Don't let the world around you squeeze you into its own mold" (Romans 12:2; Phillips). Biblical revelation summons us to defy many of the basic values of our materialistic, adulterous society.

But that is impossible! At least for isolated individuals. It is simply not possible for isolated believers to resist the anti-Christian values which pour forth from our radios, TV's, and billboards. Tragically, affluent church buildings and ecclesiastical lifestyles subtly reinforce the same sinful values of our secular society. The values of our affluent society seep slowly and subtly into our hearts and minds. The only way to defy them is to immerse ourselves so deeply in Christian fellowship that God can fundamentally remold our thinking as we find our primary identity with other brothers and sisters in Christ who are also unconditionally committed to biblical values.

Christian fellowship means unconditional availability to and unlimited liability for the other sisters and brothers—emotionally, financially, and spiritually. In the early church, when one member suffered, they all suffered. When one rejoiced, they all rejoiced (1 Corinthians 12:26). When a person or church experienced economic trouble, the others shared without reservation. And when a brother or sister fell into sin, the others gently restored the straying person. The sisters and brothers were available to each other, liable for each other, and accountable to each other.

According to the New Testament, being part of Christ's body means being unconditionally available and totally liable for the other sisters and brothers. The problem is that churches in North America are not structured to help us do that.

I think we need to break down large congregations of more than 100 persons into small weekly home meetings of 15-25 people. All the small groups should still come together once a week for a common service of teaching, celebration, and worship, but the heart of the church should be the small home meetings.

It is in that kind of setting—and perhaps only in that kind of setting—that the church today will be able to forge a faithful lifestyle for Christians in an Age of Hunger. In small house-church settings, brothers and sisters can challenge each others' affluent lifestyles. They can discuss family finances and evaluate each others' annual budgets. Larger purchases (like houses, cars, and long vacations) can be evaluated honestly in terms of the needs of both the individuals involved and God's poor around the world. Tips for simple living can be shared. Voting patterns that liberate the poor, jobs that are ecologically responsible, charitable donations that build self-reliance among the oppressed and direct action campaigns that successfully challenge unjust multinational corporations—these and many other issues can be discussed openly and honestly by persons who have pledged themselves to be brothers and sisters in Christ to each other.

My second proposal on the church begins with the assumption that it is a tragic farce for the church to ask Washington to legislate what it cannot persuade Christians to live.

If we had time to examine what the Bible says about economic relationships among the people of God, we would discover that over and over again God specifically commanded His people to live together in community in such a way that they would avoid extremes of wealth and poverty—that is the point of the Old Testament legislation on the Jubilee, the Sabbatical Year, tithing, gleaning, and loans. Jesus, our only perfect model, shared a common purse with the new community of His disciples. The first church in Jerusalem and Paul in his collection were implementing what the Old Testament and Jesus had commanded. Compare that with the contemporary church.

Present economic relationships in the worldwide body of Christ are unbiblical, sinful, a hindrance to evangelism, and a desecration of the body and blood of Jesus Christ. The dollar value of the food North Americans throw in the garbage each year equals about one fifth of the total annual income of Africa's 120 million Christians. It is a sinful abomination for a small fraction of the world's Christians living in the Northern Hemisphere to grow richer year by year while our brothers and sisters in

Christ in the Third World ache and suffer for lack of minimal health care, minimal education, and even—in thousands and thousands of cases—just enough food to escape starvation.

We are like the rich Corinthian Christians who feasted without sharing their food with the poor members of the church (1 Corinthians 11:20-29). Like them we fail today to discern the reality of the one worldwide body of Christ. The tragic consequence is that we profane the body and blood of the Lord Jesus we worship. Christians in the United States spent $5.7 billion on new church construction alone in the six years from 1967 to 1972. Would we go on building lavishly furnished expensive church plants and adding air conditioning, new rugs, and organs if members of our congregation were starving?

Churches need to adopt more simple corporate lifestyles. Virtually all church construction today is unnecessary. Four large congregations could share every church building if one group would worship on Friday evening, two on Sunday morning, and one on Sunday evening (the four congregations of Dallas' Fellowship Bible Church do that). Significantly simpler personal and ecclesiastical lifestyles would make assistance for economic development possible on an astonishingly increased scale.

We have seen that an Age of Hunger demands simplicity both in our personal lives and in our churches. But compassion and simple living apart from structural change in secular society may be little more than a gloriously irrelevant ego-trip or the proud pursuit of personal purity.

Eating less beef or even becoming a vegetarian will not necessarily feed one starving child. If millions of

Americans reduce their beef consumption, but do not act politically to change public policy, the result will not necessarily be less starvation in the Third World.

Now, of course, if Christian churches live more simply and give some of the money saved to agencies promoting rural development in poor nations, then the result will be significantly less hunger. But at the same time that we change the lifestyle of our families and our churches, we must also seek justice in the public arena. Our Age of Hunger demands structural change.

I am aware that this is an exceedingly complex subject, and I don't pretend to be an expert in international economics. But a few things are becoming rather clear. Present patterns of international trade need to be changed. Industrialized nations should lower import restrictions on manufactured goods from poor nations. The U.S. ought to take the lead in establishing a large international grain reserve. The U.S. ought to expand its economic assistance (given through multilateral channels like the U.N.) for agricultural development among the poorest billion in our world. In 1949 at the height of the Marshall plan, the U.S. gave 2.79 percent of GNP in foreign aid. Today we are twice as rich but we give only .25 percent—1/11 as large a percentage!

But who would profit from such changes? Tragically, many Third World countries are ruled by wealthy elites who use their limited foreign exchange to buy luxury goods from the developed world. But that does not mean that we can wash our hands of the whole problem. Many of these governments remain in power because they receive massive military aid and diplomatic support from the United States and other industrial nations. The United States has trained large numbers of police who have tortured thousands of people working for social justice in countries like Chile and Brazil. Multinational corporations in the United States work very closely with the repressive governments. Events in Brazil and Chile demonstrate that the United States will support dictatorships that use torture and do little for the poorest one half as long as these regimes are friendly to U.S. investments.

What can be done? U.S. citizens must demand a drastic reorientation of U.S. foreign policy. We must demand a foreign policy that unequivocally sides with the poor. If we believe that "all men are created equal," then our foreign policy must be redesigned to promote the interests of all people and not just the wealthy elites in developing countries and our own multinational corporations. We should use our economic and diplomatic power to push for change in Third World dictatorships, especially those like Brazil and Chile that make widespread use of torture. We should insist that foreign aid go only to countries seriously committed to improving the lot of the poorest portions of the population. We should openly encourage nonviolent movements working for structural change in developing countries. U.S. foreign policy ought to encourage justice rather than injustice. Only then will proposed changes in international trade and foreign aid actually improve the lot of the poorest billion.

These questions are uncomfortable and upsetting. I sometimes wish that discipleship and peacemaking had less to do with my economic lifestyle and the economics of affluent Western nations. But they do intersect. So I am forced to make up my mind on two simple interrelated questions: Do I really believe that Jesus is Lord? Do I want to fall into theological liberalism?

Our most fundamental Christian confession is that Jesus is Lord. But He won't be Lord of our family life and allow radio and TV commercials to be Lord of our family budget and multinational corporations to be Lord of our business practices. If Jesus is our Lord, then He must be Lord of our business practices, our economic lifestyle, Lord of our entire life.

The Historic Peace Churches are a biblical people who have opposed theological liberalism. But still I'm afraid that we are in danger of falling into theological liberalism today. We usually think of theological liberalism in connection with issues like the bodily resurrection and the deity of Jesus Christ. And that is correct. Theological liberals have fallen into terrible heresy in recent times by rejecting those basic doctrines of historic Christianity. But notice why that happened. Modern people became so impressed with modern science that they thought they could no longer believe in the miraculous. So they discarded the supernatural aspects of Christianity and abandoned the resurrection and the divinity of Christ.[5] They allowed the values of surrounding society rather than biblical truth to shape their thinking and acting. That is the essence of theological liberalism. In our time, we are in desperate danger of repeating exactly the same mistake in the whole area of justice and the poor. We are allowing surrounding society rather than Scripture to shape our values and life. Have not our economic lifestyles and our attitudes toward the poor been shaped more by our affluent materialistic society than by Scripture—even though the Bible says as much about this set of issues as it does about the atonement or Christology?

If we want to escape theological liberalism, if our confession that Jesus is Lord is genuine, then we must cast aside the secular economic values of our materialistic society. Now I know many of the people in our churches don't want to do that. They don't want to hear the Bible's radical call to costly discipleship. But that simply raises in a more painful way for every church leader the basic question: Is Jesus really our Lord?

Many pastors, Sunday school superintendents, and other church leaders agree that we should be concerned with the poor and work for peace via justice. They are willing to talk carefully about these things as long as the message is not too upsetting to the congregation, as long as it does not offend potential new members and hinder church growth. But they don't make it clear, as Jesus did, that we really have to choose between Jesus and Mammon. They are afraid to teach and preach the clear biblical word that economic systems perpetrate institutionalized violence and murder because that would offend business people. One wonders whether it is Jesus or church growth, whether it is Jesus or vocational security, whether it is Jesus or social acceptance who finally is our Lord.

There are very few church traditions as helpful as that of the Historic Peace Churches for enabling us to understand and live out the proper relationship between peacemaking and economics. Simplicity in both personal lifestyles and church life has been a part of our heritage for centuries. We of all people ought to be able to hear the God of the poor calling us today to more simple lifestyles. But one only needs to look at the vast wealth and affluent lifestyles among our people to see that this generation is abandoning that heritage at an incredibly rapid pace. Our parents and grandparents still understood the basic biblical call for separation from the sinful materialistic values of surrounding society even though at times they applied it in a superficial legalistic way. But will there be any heritage of simplicity left to pass on to our children?

The following story illustrates the problem. Last summer a Presbyterian couple came to a Families for Justice Retreat I was leading. During the course of the weekend, they shared their agonizing difficulty in communicating their concern for a simple lifestyle with their teenage son. They explained that he went to a Christian high school where all his friends had their own cars with nicely remodeled interiors and cassette players. Naturally he wanted a car for himself. Each family drove two or three cars to church on Sunday. Rather than helping them communicate biblical values to their son, the Christian high school and even the church were subtly instilling the materialistic values of surrounding society.

Then the couple explained that their son was attending a Mennonite high school. They explained that they had left the Presbyterian Church and joined a Mennonite Church in order to find support for their commitment to simple living. To their dismay, they discovered that most of the Mennonites there were rushing madly in the other direction. I have reflected a lot about that couple. Does that story provide the basic clue about where we are going?

Is Jesus or surrounding society our Lord? If we intend to follow the risen One, then I think we will discover that He calls us to be peacemakers through economic change—through more simple personal economic lifestyles, through more simple church lifestyles, and through action designed to change economic systems that produce violence by statute.

Discussion Questions

1. What is structural injustice?
2. What biblical evidence is there that participation in structural injustice is as sinful as committing personal sins?
3. How are North Americans involved in structural injustice today?
4. Does changing our personal lifestyles and the corporate lifestyle of the church contribute to peace in the world? Why are these two things inadequate by themselves?
5. What is the essence of theological liberalism? Is it present in your church?
6. Should those who are opposed to war be equally concerned about the violence done by unjust economic structure? What would that mean for you and your church?

4
Walking in the
Resurrection in a
Violent World

Walking in the Resurrection in a Violent World

Each Sunday affluent North American Christians gather in the richest society on earth to worship the God of the poor. We gather together as secure North Americans who fail to incarnate our nonviolent words in costly action, thus contradicting our alleged commitment to the One whose nonviolent way was inseparable from the terror and agony of the cross. That's the bad news of this short sermon.

But there is also good news. We also gather as people who know that the risen Lord Jesus has already won the decisive victory over the powers of injustice, war, and destruction. And therefore we want to rededicate ourselves to daring, costly action in the war of the Lamb who will reign forever as King of kings and Lord of lords.

But before we can rejoice in the good news, we must honestly face the bad news. Much of this bad news already was noted in chapter three. The affluence we enjoy is possible in part because of violent structures which enrich us and starve others. Last year the National

Academy of Sciences reported that "750 million people in the poorest nations live in extreme poverty with annual incomes of less than $75." According to the United Nations, at least 462 million people were actually starving a few years ago and recent reports indicate that has not changed. We North Americans, on the other hand, live as wealthy aristocrats. According to a recent sophisticated study by a University of Pennsylvania economist, the average person in the U.S. is 14 times as rich as the average person in India. We consume five times as much grain as the average person in Asia.

Unfortunately it is not just that we are astronomically affluent while others are desperately poor. To a significant extent, their poverty results from our affluence. Now, of course, we must be careful not to overstate the case. North Americans are not responsible for all the poverty in the world. Greedy elites in Third World countries and ancient religious and cultural patterns also make their callous contribution to death by starvation. But we must come to grips with the way that economic structures help create affluence here and poverty abroad.

If we are honest about the contemporary economic scene, we cannot fail to hear a divine summons to action. At every level of church life from the local congregation to conference commissions to colleges and seminaries, we need to devote vast new quantities of time and resources to a biblical analysis of structural injustice in our world. And we also need a burst of creative exploration of new ways to use economic and political power (in ways that are faithful to kingdom values) to promote more just national and international socioeconomic structures.

But a vastly strengthened concern for structural change will not weaken our historic concern for faithful personal lifestyles within the redeemed community of the people of God. If we take seriously the model of the incarnate Son who became a slave to redeem us, then we will not wait to begin living simple personal lifestyles until we have changed economic structures. Simple personal lifestyles are extremely important now—both as visible albeit imperfect models pointing to the coming kingdom and as an authentication of our call to government for sweeping systemic change.

The other part of the bad news we must face is that we have talked about peace and then gladly enjoyed the fruits of violence. Claiming to believe that it is the peacemakers who are blessed, we have to a terrible degree happily accepted the benefits of a violent status quo. We preached peace and then eagerly moved into Indian lands as a violent North American society destroyed Indian tribe after Indian tribe in its bloody march across the continent. We urged nonresistance on our black sisters and brothers even though precious few of us took a costly, courageous stand against racist structures. We teach nonviolence today to third world converts while we continue to enjoy and sometimes even defend the violent status quo in the international economic order that enables us to grow fat while others starve. We deserve the biting, sarcastic indictment of black theologian James Cone: "There is an ugly contrast between the sweet, nonviolent language of white Christians and their participation in a violently unjust system." We have no right to call others to the way of peace, indeed we have no right to claim we believe in the way of peace at all unless we do so out of identification with the oppressed of the earth.

Biblical nonviolence can be lived and taught only in a

context of genuine identification and involvement with the oppressed. It is clear both ideologically and theologically that the call for nonviolence is a faithless reactionary support for the status quo when it is issued by the oppressors to the oppressed. Tragically, that is the way we North American peace churches have too often done it. To be sure, we did not always make that mistake. When we first dared to preach and live the glorious gospel of peace, we did it as relatively powerless sixteenth, seventeenth, and eighteenth-century folk ready to be martyred by the establishment.

Our biblical roots should never have allowed us to forget what we knew then. When God became flesh to redeem the world by loving His enemies, He "emptied himself, taking the form of a servant ... and ... humbled himself and became obedient unto death ... on a cross " (Philippians 2:7-8). When Jesus came preaching peace, He did not come as an aristocratic Sadducee or a powerful Roman governor. He did not come as a Roman oppressor and then call on the oppressed to love Him and His imperialist friends. He came as a member of the oppressed class to live and teach loving nonviolence to all people. He became flesh as an oppressed Person, and as He called on the oppressed to love their oppressors, He also demanded such sweeping economic changes that the oppressors crucified Him. That way the message has integrity.

And only that way does it have integrity. Unless the Historic Peace Churches living in affluent North America are prepared to engage in a sweeping identification with the oppressed of the earth that goes far beyond sharing a few million surplus dollars and a handful of committed sons and daughters for the cause of relief and development, we should forget it. We should admit to ourselves and the world that our silent support of the unjust status quo is a thundering denial of our peace testimony. We should admit that we have joined Caesar and forsaken the incarnate One who lives among the poor of the earth.

But we need not despair. There is also good news. The gospel is *still* true. God still loves His enemies. God still loves sinners. God still loves even us in spite of our tragically mixed history of daring obedience and dreadful failure. "But God shows his love for us in that while we were yet sinners Christ died for us. ... For if while we were enemies we were reconciled to God by the death of his Son, much more, now that we are reconciled, shall we be saved by his life" (Romans 5:8-10). God in Christ tenderly accepts you and me as we are and forgives us for our past neglect, timidity, and omission. We *are* reconciled to God as we believe in Christ on the cross.

Furthermore, the text says that we shall be saved by His life. Paul means by Jesus' resurrection. Christ "was put to death for our trespasses and raised for our justification" (Romans 4:25)—raised in order that we might be made righteous by the grace of God. We don't have to try to live the costly life of nonviolence by ourselves. We can live nonviolently because we walk in the resurrection. The same supernatural power of God that raised Jesus from the dead now blows through our timid, fearful personalities. It is in the power of the resurrection that we can boldly go forth to join the oppressed of the earth in their costly confrontation with the oppressor.

And it is because the tomb was empty that we know that the nonviolent way is not an impossible dream but the truth about the future. As was noted in chapter one, the resurrection was the decisive confirmation of Jesus' claims and Jesus' methods. If He had remained in the tomb, then His method of overcoming evil through suffering love would indeed have been exposed as absurd utopian naïveté. But He arose and reigns as King of kings and Lord of lords. Right now He is the Sovereign of this gloriously created, tragically corrupted, world. The resurrection assures us that the decisive victory over injustice and violence has already been won and that the completion of that victory will surely come. Because of the resurrection, we know that this whole fantastic creation will ultimately be freed from its bondage to decay and will obtain the glorious liberty of the children of God (Romans 8:19 ff.). The Spirit of the resurrected Christ at work in every believer is the firstfruits, the down payment, that unmistakably signals the final consummation.

The resurrection in fact provides the best clue about the relationship between our work for peace and justice now and the perfect shalom of the New Jerusalem. There is both continuity and discontinuity between our work now and the coming kingdom just as there was continuity and discontinuity between Jesus of Nazareth and the risen Lord Jesus. The continuity is crucial. It was Jesus of Nazareth who was raised on the third day. It was not some spiritual resurrection in the confused minds of befuddled disciples. It was the man from Nazareth who arose bodily from the tomb and appeared to talk and eat with His discouraged, frightened followers. But there was also discontinuity. The risen Jesus was no longer subject to death and decay. His resurrected body could do things we do not understand in our space-time continuum.

I believe there is the same continuity and discontinuity

between culture and history as we know it and the coming kingdom. Certainly there is discontinuity. We will not create more and more just societies until we awake some century and discover that the millennium has arrived. Dreadful imperfection will remain in persons and societies until our risen Lord Jesus returns at the Parousia to usher in the final consummation. But there is also continuity. The New Age is best described, according to Scripture, as a new *earth*, and a new *city* (Revelation 21:1, 2). It is *this* groaning creation that will be restored to wholeness (Romans 8:18-25). The tree of life in the New Jerusalem is for the healing of the *nations*. The kings of the earth will bring their glory and honor into the Holy City. (Revelation 22:1, 2).

So we work for justice and peace now, not with a naive optimism that forgets that faithfulness involves the cross, but with the solid assurance that the final word is resurrection. We have a secure faith anchored in the reality of Jesus' resurrection and a solid hope fixed on the resurrected One's ultimate restoration of the broken beauty of creation. Anchored by that faith and hope and swept along by the pulsating power of the risen Lord Jesus in our lives, we dare to rededicate ourselves to the One who calls us to costly struggle for peace through justice.

As we walk in the resurrection, there is a glorious costly future ahead for the church.

I dream of a time when thousands and thousands of congregations from the Historic Peace Churches have been transformed from comfortable clubs largely conformed to surrounding society's materialism into radical beachheads of the coming kingdom. Thousands of congregations where all relationships whether psychological, social, or economic have been so fundamentally transformed that they are visible models of the coming shalom. Congregations whose visible wholeness is so tangible and contagious that it will draw unbelievers to faith in Jesus Christ. Congregations where the question of what constitutes a faithful personal economic lifestyle is one of the top agenda items for mutual discernment and discipling. Congregations whose internal shalom authenticates their constant call for nuclear disarmament.

I dream of a time when all the centers of leadership and responsibility in our denominations proclaim with a united voice: "Sisters and brothers, if we are to be faithful to Christ and our heritage of peacemaking, we must confront the terrible reality of systemic injustice." A time when all the centers of leadership decide that it is not enough merely for our relief agencies to include development, it is not enough merely for our relief and development agencies to take some cautious steps toward justice education so that a few of the constituency will begin to understand the systemic causes of poverty. Instead, they will decide as a united leadership of conference leaders, editors, Sunday school and youth leaders, college and seminary personnel: "We must, regardless of the cost, confront our entire constituency with the nature of systemic injustice and the extent of our involvement in it." Such a move would involve terrible risk. Most of our people are rushing madly away from our heritage of simplicity. They will not hear gladly the message that our affluence results to a significant degree from sinful structures that the God of the poor abhors. But we could decide faithfully to convey that message as a united leadership. We could make that message central in our sermons, our periodicals, our Sunday school curricula, and all of our programs. We could send hundreds of teams of full-time volunteers into the churches in a massive program of justice and peace education. We could, if we dared to risk our security and leadership for the sake of faithfulness to Christ, prayerfully yet persistently insist that our people choose in this decade whom they will serve.

I dream of a time when it will be the norm rather than the exception for our people to authenticate our word about peace with lives of costly, nonviolent identification with the oppressed. For tens of thousands that will mean leaving comfortable rural or suburban surroundings to join the poor of the earth in their struggle for justice—by making our homes in the black or Spanish-speaking inner cities, in the Appalachian Highlands, in unjust third world settings. When tens of thousands of our people have done their homework so they are competent to discuss pending legislation with Senators, when tens of thousands of our people are going to jail, when we are being tortured and getting martyred in a nonviolent struggle for justice in the inner cities and the third world, then we will have the right to talk about nonviolence.

Of course, not all of us should move. For others, identifying with the oppressed will mean talking and working against unjust structures here and abroad so persistently and singlemindedly that our scholarly societies, our professional colleagues, our business associates and political friends will discover that we worship the God of the poor not success, that we will be thrown out rather than be silent, that we will accept social disgrace, professional failure, unemployment, even imprisonment for civil disobedience rather than forsake our identification with the oppressed.

I dream of a movement of biblical Christians so sensitive to the Holy Spirit's guidance and so immersed in prayer that they will know when to work within existing economic and political structures and when to build new structures. Biblical Christians so led by the living Lord that they will dare to move from reform from within to nonviolent direct action when that is the appropriate approach. Biblical Christians who will dare to pray and picket, evangelize and blockade until North Americans can no longer ignore the way our affluence is built on poverty and starvation abroad. Biblical Christians who even as they are carted off to jail will express Christlike tenderness to policemen, who even as they are sentenced will explain Jesus' way of love and justice to incredulous judges, who will even dare to risk their own lives in order to release the captives and free the oppressed. By word and sign we must witness to the principalities and powers in the affluent countries that unjust economic structures are an abomination to the Lord of the universe.

I dream of churches who will find new ways to witness to the militaristic madness of modern society. Churches where the issue is no longer over whether the peace commission's ringing resolution is appropriate since some of the membership no longer is pacifist, but rather mutual discernment about how to support those who have refused to pay war taxes. Churches where most of the total denominational membership treks to Washington to protest nuclear proliferation.

I dream of a future which will not include the nuclear disaster that I cried about with my eleven-year-old son this summer.

This August as our family drove home to Ontario for our vacation, Ted and I began talking about nuclear fission and fusion. He understands that better than I do and he loves to discuss it, so I asked him to explain it to me again. As we talked, the conversation moved to the question of nuclear weapons and Ted asked what the chance of nuclear war was. I decided he deserved an honest answer. So I explained that responsible scientists believe that there is at least a 50 percent chance of nuclear war by the time he reaches the age of 25. He became very quiet and serious and then asked: "Do you mean there is a 50 percent chance that I will die before I am twenty-five?" When I said, "Yes," he started to cry quietly and so did I. With tears in my eyes, I tried to say how terrible I felt that he lived in that kind of world. I wanted to take him in my arms to comfort him, but I was driving and he seemed to want to be alone with his thoughts.

After awhile when we started talking again, he asked me why I continued to do the things I am doing if I think everything may blow up so soon. I tried to assure him that God is in charge of history and that I am doing what I can. But his question jarred me. Am I really doing all I can to promote justice and peace in the world?

Are we really doing all God wants us to do? That is the question for each of us. Let us all rededicate ourselves to the crucified and risen Lamb and to the Lamb's war for shalom.

And now may the radical justice of God the Father, the liberating forgiveness of God the Son, and the revolutionary transforming presence of God the Holy Spirit so blow through your lives that you may go forth into this broken world and fight the Lamb's war knowing that the risen King has already won the victory over injustice, violence, and death.

Hallelujah. Amen.

Discussion Questions

1. Have Christians in the Historic Peace Churches participated in murder by privilege? If we have, why have so few of our people realized that this is the case?
2. What would we have to charge for our belief in the way of peace to be modeled after the approach of Jesus?
3. How does the resurrection relate to peace-making?
4. What steps could your congregation take to become a beachhead of Jesus' coming kingdom?
5. What five steps could you as an individual or a family take in the next month (and year) to identify with the poor and oppressed?
6. List all the things you are doing to avoid nuclear disaster. Share these with a few friends (or your Sunday school class) and ask whether they feel you are doing enough.

NOTES

Notes

Chapter 1.
The Cross and Violence

1. The following section is largely dependent on Martin Hengel, *Victory over Violence* (London: SPCK, 1975), pp. 38 ff.

2. *Ibid.*, p. 63.

3. *Ibid.*, p. 69.

4. *Ibid.*, p. 55.

5. *Ibid.*, p. 71.

6. Robert Sloan, *The Acceptable Year of the Lord* (Austin: Schola Press, 1977), pp. 43, 44.

7. *Ibid.*, pp. 168. 171.

8. Eg. W. G. Kummel, *Promise and Fulfillment* (London: SCM Press, 1957); George E. Ladd, *Jesus and the Kingdom* (New York: Harper, 1964).

9. Hengel, *Victory over Violence*, p. 80.

10. *Ibid.*, pp. 81, 112.

11. *Ibid.*, p. 82.

12. See C. E. B. Cranfield, *The Gospel According to Mark, The Cambridge Greek New Testament Commentary* (Cambridge: Cambridge University Press, 1963), pp. 441, 442 for a discussion of Jesus' response ("I am") and the synoptic parallels.

13. *Ibid.*, pp. 353, 354.

14. Hengel, *Victory over Violence*, p. 76.

15. W. F. Albright and C. S. Mann, *Matthew* "Anchor Bible" (New York: Doubleday, 1971), p. 71 and Eduard Schweizer, *The Good News According to Matthew* (Atlanta: John Knox, 1975), p. 132: "The principle 'Love your neighbor' (Lev. 19:18), to be sure, was always interpreted so as to apply to fellow Israelites, not to others."

16. Hengel, *Victory over Violence*, p. 75.

17. Schweizer, *Matthew*, p. 132.

18. Schweizer, *Matthew*, p. 194.

19. *Ibid.*, p. 130.

20. Albright and Mann, *Matthew*, p. 69.

21. Schweizer, *Matthew*, p. 130.

22. Jurgen Moltmann, *The Crucified God* (New York: Harper, 1974), pp. 125, 132.

23. *Ibid.*, p. 142.

24. Oscar Cullmann, *The Christology of the New Testament* (Philadelphia: Westminster, 1963), pp. 51-82.

25. See Cranfield, *Mark*, p. 343 for a discussion of the authenticity of this verse.

26. *Ibid.*, p. 427.

27. Dale Brown, *Brethren and Pacifism* (Elgin, Ill.: Brethren Press, 1970), p. 121.

28. Rufus H. Jones in *The Church, the Gospel and War* (New York: Harper, 1948), p. 5.

29. Thus Richard Mouw, *Politics and the Biblical Drama* (Grand Rapids: Eerdmans, 1976), pp. 112-116, is correct in arguing that Yoder is wrong in asserting that Christians must universally and consistently imitate the cross. But that does not in any way undercut Yoder's thesis that the cross is the norm for the Christian life.

30. For a short overview, see Martin Hengel, *Christ and Power* (Philadelphia: Fortress, 1977), pp. 53 ff. For a longer discussion see Roland Bainton, *Christian Attitudes Toward War and Peace* (New York: Abingdon, 1960).

Chapter 2.
Christ and Power

1. William Keeney, *Lordship as Servanthood* (Newton, Kan.: Faith and Life Press, 1975), p. 86. The classic statement of a nonresistant position is of course Guy F. Hershberger, *War, Peace, and Nonresistance* (Scottdale, Pa.: Herald Press, 1953).

2. Keeney, *Lordship as Servanthood*, p. 67.

3. Quoted in Martin Hengel, *Christ and Power* (Philadelphia: Fortress, 1977), p. 2.

4. Richard Mouw, *Politics and the Biblical Drama* (Grand Rapids: Eerdmans, 1976), p. 109.

5. After writing the following section, I discovered the excellent article by J. Lawrence Burkholder, "Nonresistance, Nonviolent Resistance, and Power," *Kingdom, Cross and Community*, ed. J. Richard Burkholder and Calvin Redekop, (Scottdale, Pa.: Herald Press, 1976), pp. 131-137.

6. W. F. Albright and C. S. Mann, *Matthew* "Anchor Bible" (Garden City: Doubleday, 1971), p. 68.

7. John Howard Yoder, *The Politics of Jesus* (Grand Rapids: Eerdmans, 1972), p. 158.

8. For the literature, see the material cited in Mouw, *Politics*, p. 86, n. 1.

9. See also Ephesians 3:10. I do not, as John Stott suggests, limit the connotation of "principalities and powers" to secular socio-political structures. See John Stott's response in my *Evangelism, Salvation and Social Justice* (Bramcote Notts, England: Grove Books, 1977), p. 24.

10. Naperville: Alec R. Allenson, 1960.

11. C. E. B. Cranfield, *A Commentary on Romans 12—13*, "Scottish Journal of Theology Occasional Papers, No. 12" (Edinburgh: Oliver and Boyd, 1965), p. 68.

12. Mouw, *Politics*, chapter 2.

13. Delling in *Theological Dictionary of the New Testament*, ed. Gerhard Kittel and Gerhard Friedrich, 10 vols. (Grand Rapids: Eerdmans, 1964-1976), I, 454.

14. Cf. also v. 11.

15. Albert von den Heuvel, *These Rebellious Powers* (Naperville: SCM Book Club, 1966), p. 44.

16. H. Berkhof, *Christ and the Powers* (Scottdale, Pa.: Herald Press, 1962), p. 34.

17. See my *Rich Christians in an Age of Hunger* (Downers Grove: Inter-Varsity Press, 1977), chapter 3.

18. Berkhof, *Christ and the Powers*, p. 43 and Yoder, *Politics of Jesus*, p. 152.

19. Yoder, *Politics of Jesus*, p. 204.

20. Cranfield, *Romans 12-13*, pp. 69-71.

Chapter 3.
Peacemaking and Economics

1. This chapter summarizes sections from chapters 6 to 9 of my *Rich Christians in an Age of Hunger: A Biblical Study* (Downers Grove: Inter-Varsity Press, 1977). The statistical material cited here is documented in those chapters.

2. For documentation, request the extensive supporting documentation for the superb twenty-minute filmstrip, "Guess Who's Coming to Breakfast," available from The Packard Manse Media Project, Box 450, Stoughton, Mass. 02072.

3. Jacques Ellul, *Violence* (New York: Seabury, 1969), p. 97.

4. James Douglas, *The Non-Violent Cross: A Theology of Revolution and Peace* (New York: Macmillan, 1966), p. 285.

5. See my "The Historian, The Miraculous, and Post-Newtonian Man," *Scottish Journal of Theology*, XXV (1972), 309-19; and "St. Paul's Understanding of the Nature and Significance of the Resurrection," *Novum Testamentum*, XIX (1977), 124-141.

Chapter 4.
Walking in the Resurrection
in a Violent World

1. James H. Cone, *Black Theology and Black Power* (New York: Seabury Press, 1969), p. 56.

Ronald J. Sider, a member of the Brethren in Christ Church, lives with his wife, Arbutus, and three children in the Jubilee Fellowship of Germantown, a house church in an interracial section of Philadelphia.

Sider received the PhD in history from Yale University in 1969. After teaching for ten years at the Temple University Campus of Messiah College, he became associate professor of theology at Eastern Baptist Theological Seminary in 1977.

President of Evangelicals for Social Action, Sider is convener of the Unit on Ethics and Society of the Theological Commission of the World Evangelical Fellowship, and has organized Discipleship Workshops: Focus on Justice. He also serves on the board of Mennonite Central Committee and Bread for the World.

The Christian Peace Shelf

The Christian Peace Shelf is a selection of Herald Press books and pamphlets devoted to the promotion of Christian peace principles and their applications. The editor (appointed by the Mennonite Central Committee Peace Section) and an editorial board from the Brethren in Christ Church, the General Conference Mennonite Church, the Mennonite Brethren Church, and the Mennonite Church, represent the historic concern for peace within these constituencies.

FOR SERIOUS STUDY

Abrams, Ray H. *Preachers Present Arms* (1969). The involvement of the church in three modern wars.

Durland, William R. *No King but Caesar?* (1975). A Catholic lawyer looks at Christian violence.

Enz, Jacob J. *The Christian and Warfare* (1972). The roots of pacifism in the Old Testament.

Hershberger, Guy F. *War, Peace, and Nonresistance* (Third Edition, 1969). A classic comprehensive work on nonresistance in faith and history.

Hornus, Jean-Michael. *It Is Not Lawful for Me to Fight* (1980). Early Christian attitudes toward war, violence, and the state.

Kaufman, Donald D. *What Belongs to Caesar?* (1969). Basic arguments against voluntary payment of war taxes.

Lasserre, Jean. *War and the Gospel* (1962). An analysis of Scriptures related to the ethical problem of war.

Lind, Millard C. *Yahweh Is a Warrior* (1980). The theology of warfare in ancient Israel.

Ramseyer, Robert L. *Mission and the Peace Witness* (1979). Implications of the biblical peace testimony for the evangelizing mission of the church.

Sider, Ronald J. *Christ and Violence* (1979). A sweeping reappraisal of the church's teaching on violence.

Trocmé, André. *Jesus and the Nonviolent Revolution* (1973). The social and political relevance of Jesus.

Yoder, John H. *The Original Revolution* (1972). Essays on Christian pacifism.

_____ *Nevertheless* (1971). The varieties and shortcomings of Christian pacifism.

FOR EASY READING

Eller, Vernard. *War and Peace from Genesis to Revelation* (1981). Explores peace as a consistent theme developing throughout the Old and New Testaments.

Kaufman, Donald D. *The Tax Dilemma: Praying for Peace, Paying for War* (1978). Biblical, historical, and practical considerations on the war tax issue.

Kraybill, Donald B. *The Upside-Down Kingdom* (1978). A study of the synoptic gospels on affluence, war-making, status-seeking, and religious exclusivism.

Miller, John W. *The Christian Way* (1969). A guide to the Christian life based on the Sermon on the Mount.

Wenger, J. C. *The Way of Peace* (1977). A brief treatment on Christ's teachings and the way of peace through the centuries.

FOR CHILDREN

Bauman, Elizabeth Hershberger. *Coals of Fire* (1954). Stories of people who returned good for evil.

Moore, Ruth Nulton. *Peace Treaty* (1977). A historical novel involving the efforts of Moravian missionary Christian Frederick Post to bring peace to the Ohio Valley in 1758.

Smucker, Barbara Claassen. *Henry's Red Sea* (1955). The dramatic escape of 1,000 Russian Mennonites from Berlin following World War II.